Trinity

Trinity

The History Of An Atomic Bomb
National Historic Landmark

By
Jim Eckles

Two-second exposure from North 10,000.

ISBN-13: 978-1507798553
ISBN-10: 1507798555

Published by the Fiddlebike Partnership
Las Cruces, New Mexico 88011
Email = 19jeckles50@gmail.com

Printed by CreateSpace

Contents

Preface..VII

1. Trinity - The History of a National Historic Landmark.................1
2. Trinity Site Origins..5
3. What's Fission Got To Do With It.......................................6
4. European Physicists Contribute...7
5. Separating Atoms...8
6. The Real Start Of The Atomic Age..................................10
7. Two Bomb Designs..11
8. Trinity Site Is Needed..14
9. What's With The Name?..15
10. By Extension, The Glass Is Trinitite................................16
11. Jumbo...16
12. Building The Trinity Site Test Bed..................................19
13. Who Were The Schmidts?...21
14. Working At The Test Site..24
15. To Collect Test Data..30
16. The 100-Ton Calibration Test.......................................36
17. Jumbo's Final Role..37
18. Bomb Preparation...42
19. The Explosion..48
20. General Groves' Assessment..58
21. The Fallout And Radiation Levels..................................59
22. News Media At The Site..63
23. The Crater - A Pond Of Green Glass.............................68
24. After The War Ended..71
25. Sleeping Beauty...73
26. Trinity Site Transitions To Local Control.........................75
27. Protecting The Site...78
28. National Park Service Tries Different Tactic....................80
29. Radiation Risks At Ground Zero...................................82
30. Another Question About Safety.....................................85

31. The Radiation Numbers - How They Compare..................86
32. Open Houses...90
33. Ranch House Restoration...91
34. The 50th Anniversary..94
35. Buddhist Monks Visit...97
36. The Real Trinitite Story..98
37. Myths And Misinformation..102
38. How Trinity Generated The Roswell Incident............104
39. Trinity Adds To Controversial New Theory.................105
40. Right Or Wrong? Or Is It More Complicated?.............108
41. Trinity Site's Future..110

Additional Photos..113

Appendices
   A. Einstein's Letter to President Roosevelt....................127
   B. Schmidt Family Letters...129
   C. Marvin Davis Letters...135
   D. Carl Rudder Letters...147
   E. George Cremeens Documents....................................149

Some Sources..159

Preface

I included a Trinity Site chapter in *Pocketful Of Rockets*, my history of White Sands Missile Range. Being just one of 29 chapters, it was a bit limited. Lisa Blevins, a co-worker in Public Affairs, suggested I extract the Trinity write-up, beef it up and offer it as a separate small book. After all, there are many people interested in Trinity Site but who just don't care about the missile range. This is it.

Another reason for doing this is to keep the stories alive. Whenever I interviewed a Trinity Site veteran during one of the open houses, people would gather round. They wanted to hear what the person was saying and they wanted to hear it from a real source. That is also why I decided to include some of the letters we received from people somehow associated with Trinity Site. You can read for yourself what they had to say.

I also wanted to help fight the huge volume of misinformation and myth out there about the history and the science of Trinity Site. A lot of it is just typical American lack of understanding of most sciency things.

On the other hand, there is a lot of material obviously made up - it is just too absurd to be real. I'm not sure why someone would want to create fictional details since the real story is pretty interesting all by itself. I'm afraid you'll just have to accept that the story isn't a James Bond film and that there are no dragons or magicians involved.

I have to thank Robb Hermes, a real scientist, for trying to keep my interpretations and simplifications correct. Sometimes I mess up and those mistakes are mine, not Robb's.

Also, a salute to all the missile range personnel who, over the decades, made the public open houses possible. They worked lots of long hours, sometimes in snow, rain, heat and/or winds that blew sand so hard it blasted the paint off your car. They did excellent work handling large crowds, keeping everyone safe and allowing everyone (even the occasional kook or crazy) to experience a bit of world-changing history.

Finally, thanks to my wife Debbie who isn't interested in science but who found the people in this large story interesting. Her help while I punched keys on the computer was greatly needed and appreciated.

Jim Eckles

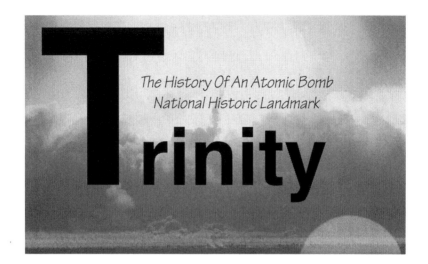

Trinity

The History Of An Atomic Bomb National Historic Landmark

As the place where the first atomic bomb was tested on July 16, 1945, most people agree that Trinity Site is a pretty important place. Those who remember the Cold War will say nuclear weapons changed the world in the blink of an eye. Although not as conspicuous as before, those weapons still color our existence.

When I worked in the White Sands Missile Range Public Affairs Office, we had a commanding general in the 80s who publicly stated Trinity Site was second only to Bethlehem in importance. Even though he would explain that the places were important for totally different reasons, I cringed every time he said it. Many must have agreed with him because he received no overt criticism from his audiences.

Many Americans don't know that the plutonium-based bomb tested at Trinity was identical to the one dropped on Nagasaki, Japan on Aug. 9, 1945 or that WWII ended just six days later when Japan's Emperor Hirohito broadcast his surrender message.

White Sands Missile Range has allowed visitors to Trinity during open houses since the 1950s. Visitors bring with them a broad assortment of backgrounds - everything from World War II vets to young families to motorcycle gang members to new age spiritualists to school science groups – and they are preloaded with a smorgasbord of opinions reflecting their upbringing, education, cultural encounters and generation.

When they get to the national historic landmark, some are disappointed there is so little to see. At ground zero (GZ) there is an obelisk marking the exact spot where the bomb was exploded. A bit of rebar sticks out of the ground marking one of the tower legs that supported the bomb. In the parking lot is what remains of Jumbo and, after a short bus ride, visitors can see the Schmidt/McDonald ranch house.

Trinity Site is so obviously important the National Park Service proposed making it a national monument in 1946 and many times thereafter. Since it was on the north end of the newly established White Sands Proving Ground, the Department of Army declined the offer and continues to reject any attempts that might change who would control the area.

I worked my first Trinity Site open house in October 1977 when the missile range only opened the site to the public once a year – on the first Saturday in October. Since then I have worked most of the open houses and continue to do so even after my retirement in 2007. I have seen tens of thousands of people wander around the site.

Between the open houses we also took special groups and individuals to Trinity. This included news media types like Walter Cronkite when he was doing the CBS nightly news and lots and lots of Japanese reporters. We also took in military leaders, scientists, Boy Scouts, school groups, historical societies, and many of the men who worked that test in 1945. Basically, any group that seemed to have a legitimate interest in the site or someone important enough could catch a special tour if a public affairs specialist was available and test missions didn't interfere. I did a lot of them.

Probably the most famous person I escorted to the site was Cronkite on Oct. 21, 1978. At least he was famous at the time as one of the most respected news anchors in the country.

It was a chilly and windy day. As you may recall, he had that thin wispy hair on top. At Trinity Site his crew had a terrible time keeping those strands of hair in place. I swear they used most of a can of hairspray to get it stuck down for his stand-up at the obelisk.

These tours between open houses were sometimes fun and sometimes about as interesting as watching paint dry. I've run a Geiger counter for Japanese TV, unlocked and locked gates for many photographers (to include Japan's version of *Playboy* magazine) and spent long days waiting for sunset photo opportunities or for complete darkness so star tracks around the obelisk could be captured on one negative.

An advantage to doing these tours was the opportunity get out from behind a desk and into the desert, to do something different. The extra long hours were usually worth it as I gathered many new experiences.

For example, I escorted a San Francisco television crew that was freaked out by the site. They weren't bothered by the radiation or anything else to do with the test. Instead, they were amazed at the lack of noise, at the solitude of the place as we waited for sunset at GZ. They said, being from a big city, they were never ever without background noise of some sort.

One television crew I escorted was shooting for a British "sciency" program called Mark Williams' Big Bangs. Mark Williams, the actor who played Mr. Weasley in the Harry Potter movies, was the presenter. It was a small operation and was easy to see why only four episodes were produced.

In addition to the typical stand-ups at the site with Williams explaining what happened there, they went to some effort to explain how a nuclear chain reaction works. To do this they tried to recreate "mousetrap fission" at Ground Zero.

This is a very popular demonstration used in many educational settings. There are many different versions of the experiment and accompanying videos on the internet. It involves setting out a large grid of armed mousetraps, each with one or two table tennis balls on top. Then a single ball is dropped onto the grid and all hell breaks lose as balls and mousetraps start flying about, triggering more and more traps. Depending on the size of the grid it is usually over in a second or two.

Williams and crew eventually got a small grid assembled, without balls, in the sand at GZ and did get a small chain reaction, but it was far from the educational ones found on line. In fact, it probably demonstrated chaos theory more than anything, as the mousetraps seemed to randomly release after they were set in place and cause us to start over in rearming them.

One special request we had for a Trinity Site visit I'm sorry we weren't able to do. In 2004, I received a call from a producer at VH1, the cable music network. Out of the blue, he asked if it might be possible for the network to film a free U2 (the Irish rock band fronted by Bono) concert at Trinity Site in conjunction with the group's new album release. He didn't offer why they wanted to use Trinity.

I was taken by surprise but gathered my wits and pointed out it was in the middle of nowhere with no hard power for miles. Having been to a few rock concerts, I knew they would need lots and lots of electricity for big sound and big lighting. It didn't seem to discourage him. He said they would bring everything.

I added there was no way we could handle any kind of a big crowd (I was imagining 25,000 attendees for a "free" event, maybe more). That didn't bother him either. He said White Sands could tell them how many people would be allowed in.

I then said we would have to do some thinking about it and would call him back. I immediately did a search on the web and learned U-2 was preparing to release their new album in November. It was going to be called *How to Dismantle an Atomic Bomb*. The proverbial light bulbs went on when I saw the title.

When I told the rest of the office, we had a good laugh. Then I called him back to tell him it wasn't going to work. I said such a request would end up in the Pentagon itself, and we didn't see the current administration approving such a venture. That was the last we heard of it. It would have been a fun event to work.

I once escorted Japanese photojournalist Toyosaki Hiromitsu to the site. A photo of me opening the Trinity gates ended up in the December 1980 issue of Japan's version of *Playboy* magazine - what a great conversation piece that is. The copy he sent me is pretty dog-eared as everyone at White Sands wanted to see it.

However, my favorite Trinity tour was on April 24, 1997 when I escorted two buses of astronomers to the site. They belonged to the International Astronomers Union that was holding a conference in Socorro on radio emissions from "galactic and extragalactic compact sources." They were in Socorro because it is the closest city to the Very Large Array Radio Telescope out on the Plains of San Augustin.

The field of antennas at the Very Large Array Radio Telescope, west of Socorro. The facility often holds open houses to coincide with Trinity Site open houses. Image courtesy of NRAO/AUI and NRAO.

I always liked this kind of group because I never had to explain the science behind nuclear fission. They understood the science. All they needed was the history.

This group looked like it was going to be extra special. Just weeks before the event, we found a website predicting that an alien spacecraft would land at Trinity Site the same day as the tour to make first official contact with the human race.

It was great. I was going to be at GZ literally and figuratively for a cosmic convergence. There would be dozens of astronomers from all over the world at Trinity ready to meet the aliens in their first-ever ceremonial landing.

Or was there more to it? Might the astronomers have already known about the landing? When I called Dave Finley, my contact at the Very

Large Array Radio Telescope, he said he knew nothing about aliens and categorically denied "extragalactic compact sources" might be alien space ships.

To say the least, the aliens didn't show. They may have been held up in traffic and we were all greatly disappointed. More than likely the landing announcement was secretly posted by one of the conference organizers to boost attendance for the bus tour to Trinity Site.

Trinity Site Origins

The Trinity Site story begins in the turmoil of the 1930s. It was a time of great political chaos and violence as authoritarian governments put into practice primitive ideas about the superiority of some races and their god-given right to subjugate whole groups of human beings. They weren't afraid to carry these views to the extremes of enslaving whole populations and marking some races for utter extinction. It was a time of incredible suffering and mass graves.

At the same time, the Great Depression was stifling the world economy and people worldwide scrambled to find their next meal. The weather even contributed as drought triggered huge dust storms in America's Southwest after decades of poor farming practices left nothing to anchor the soil. The wind blew away valuable topsoil and turned it into choking blizzards of dust blotting out the sun. It was dubbed the "Dust Bowl" or "Dirty Thirties."

Also in the 30s, physics was making headlines as scientists around the world made huge strides in doing the laboratory experiments necessary to prove various theories about the nature of the subatomic world.

In 1932, Englishman James Chadwick discovered neutrons inside atoms. Physicists around the world quickly realized the neutron, without a positive or negative charge, could penetrate all the way to an atom's nucleus without being repelled. It was thought a neutron might actually split an atom into smaller pieces.

In an Italian lab in 1934, Enrico Fermi successfully split uranium atoms using neutrons - he just didn't realize it at the time.

In December 1938, Otto Hahn and Fritz Strassmann, working in Germany, bombarded uranium atoms with neutrons and came up with evidence of a lighter element, barium, as a result of their activity. With the help of Lise Meitner and Otto Frisch, they realized they had broken apart uranium atoms with the resulting pieces being less complex elements with lower atomic numbers. They used the term "fission" to describe the process.

When atomic fission occurs some of the energy holding the nucleus together is released. At the level of a single atom this is hard to detect, but multiply it by millions and billions of times and in the blink of an eye you have an atomic bomb explosion.

In 1939, physicists around the world looked at the structure of uranium and started crunching the numbers. In January 1939, Fermi met with legendary Danish physicist Neils Bohr to discuss the possibility of a nuclear chain reaction. They quickly came to the conclusion that chain reactions might be slow moving and could continuously produce low levels of energy to generate electricity. Or they might be sudden uncontrolled reactions that release energy in a quick burst like no one had ever seen before.

What's Fission Got To Do With It

Although there can be chain reactions running at different speeds, the principles are the same. The idea is that a neutron can strike the nucleus of an element, like uranium-235, and cause the core or nucleus to split.

When the nucleus splits, in addition to the enormous release of energy, two or more neutrons are ejected. These two neutrons then split two more atoms and, in the next step, we have four neutrons flying out to split four atoms. In the next step there are eight neutrons in play, then 16, then 32 and so on. This doubling quickly grows into the millions and billions.

If each of these neutrons strike and split neighboring atoms and so on through a continuous series of divisions, there is exponential growth – it grows faster and faster. In an atomic bomb, this reaction is uncontrolled and happens in a fraction of a second. In a nuclear reactor, the chain reaction is controlled or maintained at a certain level, so the output of energy is steady instead of an instantaneous spike and decline.

Maintaining a steady chain reaction is accomplished by absorbing some of the neutrons so they cannot split atoms and expand the reaction.

Only a few elements will sustain the uncontrolled chain reaction required for an atomic bomb. Uranium-235, an isotope of uranium, is the only naturally occurring element that is fissionable.

An isotope like U-235 is a form of the element that behaves the same chemically but differs in a radioactivity sense. For instance, uranium-238 (the number refers to its atomic weight or mass and also is its number of protons and neutrons added together) is the most common form of the element found in nature. In fact more than 99.2 percent of all uranium is the 238 form. Uranium-235 accounts for only .7 of one percent, but it is the form necessary for a bomb.

Both forms have 92 protons in their nuclei and 92 electrons in the outer shells to balance the core's positive charge. This means that in a chemical reaction such as exposure to the air (oxidation), the different isotopes will behave the same.

The difference is that uranium-238 has 146 neutrons in the nucleus while the 235 version only has 143 neutrons. This makes uranium-235 less stable, easier to split and, as a result, more radioactive.

The term "enrichment" is used to describe the process of increasing the percentage of U-235 present in a mix of various uranium isotopes. The term "depleted uranium" (DU) refers to uranium with the U-235 removed, leaving a dense, hard metal that has been used in some conventional weapons and armor plate. Civilian uses run the gamut from boat keels to coloring in dentures.

Until recently, the element uranium was considered very rare. It turns out it is more abundant than tin, silver or mercury. It is about as common as arsenic. It is much more dense than lead but not as dense as gold.

From the end of World War II through the 50s, there was a uranium boom in America. Prospectors armed with Geiger counters swarmed through the West, especially in the Four Corners area, because uranium is found in sandstone. The boom was large enough to appear as a plot line in movies and television. In 1956, *Uranium Boom* and *Dig That Uranium* with the Bowery Boys both made it to movie houses.

In 1958, an episode of the *Lucy-Desi Comedy Hour* on CBS was titled "Lucy Hunts Uranium." Set in Las Vegas and the surrounding desert, the Lucy regulars with Fred MacMurray in tow set out to strike it rich looking for uranium. To say the least it is a "screwball comedy."

European Physicists Contribute

By the late 1930s, many of the brightest and best scientists from Europe had fled German and Italian tyranny. Men like Albert Einstein, Edward Teller and Hans Bethe went to the United States while others took positions in Britain.

Enrico Fermi was awarded the Nobel Prize in 1938 and used the event to escape Mussolini's regime in Italy. His wife was Jewish and he feared for her safety as well as the rest of the family.

He took his family with him to Stockholm where he was awarded the prize in physics on Dec. 10, 1938. At the end of the month he sailed, with his family, to the United States returning to Italy only as a visitor after the war. When he got to the United States in early 1939, he reportedly said he was establishing the American branch of the Fermi family.

Enrico Fermi

Leo Szilard was a Hungarian physicist who initially fled to Britain but then moved on to the United States in 1938. While officials in America didn't take much notice of the nuclear possibilities budding in the world's physics laboratories, refugees like Szilard had the vision to see a dim future if Hitler built an atomic bomb first. To him it was a scary situation that meant hellfire and Nazi domination for the entire planet.

Working with Hungarian physicists Edward Teller and Eugene Wigner, Szilard drafted a letter to President Roosevelt warning him of the possibility of atomic bombs and of Germany's scientific capability to do the research and build them. He said a single one of these bombs placed in a ship might destroy a whole·port and much of the city around it.

Szilard realized the U.S. government probably wouldn't pay much attention to him, so he convinced his old friend Albert Einstein, the most famous scientist alive, to sign the letter.

The letter was signed on Aug. 2, 1939, but didn't get to the president until Oct. 11. It did not create an immediate sensation. One can imagine the staff of advisors and military commanders scratching their heads wondering what Szilard was hinting at in the letter. It was well beyond their everyday experiences and required someone with some science knowledge and the imagination to see the possibilities. See Appendix A for the text of Einstein's letter.

An advisory committee was formed with almost no budget to look into the matter. The government didn't share its work with the immigrant scientists and to them it looked like nothing was happening. Because of this apparent disregard of their warning, the European physicists voluntarily censored their work. They were afraid that publishing any additional experimental work would only be advantageous to the Germans.

Separating Atoms

In 1940, the government's committee slogged through past research and conducted some original research to see if Szilard was right. After all, this was a government project that didn't have a high priority yet. They wanted to make sure good money wasn't going to be wasted based on some theoretical scientific mumbo jumbo.

By the end of the year, one report to the committee stated gaseous diffusion could successfully separate U-235 from its more common brother, U-238. This method would use uranium in a gaseous form and force the gas through a series of fine filters. The larger U-238 atoms would eventually be filtered out by the barriers while the smaller U-235 atoms passed through to be collected after thousands of passes – an atom at a time.

To put into perspective how tedious this process would be, the ratio of U-238 to U-235 is about 138 to one. To get one atom of U-235, the process has to discard 138 atoms of waste U-238.

In May 1941, a positive report was prepared concluding that an atomic bomb was possible and it could be built in a reasonable amount of time.

In October 1941, President Roosevelt gave the approval to build a bomb. On December 6, the day before the Japanese Pearl Harbor attack, he signed the document to establish the Manhattan Project that would oversee research, design and construction of the bomb.

In December, scientists and engineers started looking into using another method, an electromagnetic process, to separate the U-235 from U-238. In this process, a cluster of raw uranium ions would be accelerated around the curves of a racetrack in a magnetic field. The heavier U-238 atoms, since they have more mass, would fly a little further out in making the turn. The lighter U-235 atoms would make a tighter turn and could be picked off – an atom at a time.

Much the same thing happens on a NASCAR track. At the same speed, a lightweight stock car would carve a path much tighter in the turns compared to a stock SUV.

The Oak Ridge Y-12 or electromagnetic racetrack for separating the two uranium isotopes. Tons of silver from the U.S. reserves were used in making the magnets. Oak Ridge photo.

Once the United States was officially in the war in December 1941, things started to move with more urgency and with more money to propel it. In September 1942, Leslie Groves was appointed head of the Manhattan Project and was promoted to brigadier general to give him the clout necessary for such a job. In October, Groves appointed Robert Oppenheimer to head the scientific research needed to build the bomb.

Together Groves and Oppenheimer picked the old Los Alamos Boys Ranch in northern New Mexico as the headquarters for bomb research. In the spring of 1943 work started at Los Alamos. Oppenheimer had spent time at the ranch as a boy so he was familiar with it and the area.

The Real Start Of The Atomic Age?

Meanwhile, on December 2, 1942, Enrico Fermi provided large-scale, dramatic proof that fission was the real deal by creating the first controlled atomic chain reaction. It was a clear demonstration of why he earned a Nobel Prize. For his experiment, Fermi and his team built the first nuclear reactor in a squash court under the football stadium at the University of Chicago.

They built the reactor, or "pile" as some called it, out of graphite blocks - over 350 tons of the slick stuff. Graphite has the ability to slow down and diffuse neutrons. This was used to prevent a sudden, unexpected spike in the chain reaction that might accelerate so quickly they would not have time to respond. With the graphite slowing everything down to a human scale, Fermi could monitor the slow ramp-up of the chain reaction and restrain it to a safe continuous level.

Spaces were dug out of the blocks to accept lumps of uranium oxide placed inside the structure to fuel the reaction. Over 90,000 pounds of uranium was used. It was the natural mixture of U-235 and U-238.

Holes were also drilled so cadmium control rods could be inserted into the pile to act as emergency brakes. Cadmium can absorb huge numbers of slow neutrons, so with the rods inside the pile, it was just that - a pile of components not doing much. Many neutrons were absorbed by the rods while other neutrons were not splitting atoms fast enough to sustain a chain reaction.

As the men built the pile, they created a critical mass of uranium because of the amount and its density. As they stacked the blocks and placed the uranium, the cadmium prevented the radioactive mass from taking off in an uncontrolled chain reaction.

Later, after the reactor was completed, by removing the cadmium rods the neutrons were not absorbed but were free to smash into uranium atoms and split them, releasing more neutrons to split other atoms.

Fermi had made such meticulous calculations, all but one cadmium rod was easily removed to get to the point where the chain reaction was notable. Then, as Fermi monitored his instruments, the last rod was removed a few inches at a time until he was satisfied he had the reactor running at a very low and safe level. He had precise control and there was never any danger of a runaway reaction.

Even though Fermi ran the reactor for less than 30 minutes, it was a clear demonstration validating many of the ideas postulated at the time. In fact, many experts say the Atomic Age really began in that squash court in 1942, a couple of years before the first atomic bomb test at Trinity

Site. They would argue the bomb was simply the next technological step and was a forgone conclusion after Fermi's test. Of course, the bomb test turned out to be a hugely more spectacular starting point and one that resonates with people.

Two Bomb Designs

In 1943, construction was underway at Oak Ridge, Tennessee to build the various separation plants needed to gather U-235. Later in the year construction started at Hanford, Washington for the first nuclear reactor designed to run continuously. Hanford also saw the construction of a reactor in early 1945 for the sole purpose of producing plutonium, another element capable of fission like U-235.

Plutonium is a man-made element and was discovered in 1940 when samples of uranium were bombarded with neutrons as if they were in a reactor. Scientists discovered some of the uranium (U-238) was "transmuted" into another element, neptunium, which immediately decayed or broke down into another element, plutonium.

The first sizeable batches of plutonium were created in an early reactor built at Oak Ridge. Enough was made to do tests and characterize its radioactive profile. Scientists quickly discovered plutonium would work in an atomic bomb.

However, there was a catch to using plutonium in making a bomb. In April 1944, Emilio Segre, an Italian Jew who fled Europe before the war, analyzed some of the plutonium from the Oak Ridge reactor while working at Los Alamos. He discovered plutonium would not work in the bomb they were devising for U-235. Calculations showed such a bomb design using plutonium would be a low-yield fizzle. Another design would be needed to use plutonium.

Early on, scientists and engineers under Oppenheimer's leadership at Los Alamos were planning a gun-type design for the U-235 bomb. In a theoretical sense the design was utter simplicity. Of course, the engineering details were anything but.

It called for using high explosives to propel one piece of non-critical U-235 down a tube to strike another piece. When they met, the sub-critical pieces would come together to form a single critical mass that would fission immediately.

For an excruciatingly detailed look at the design of both bombs, get a copy of *Atom Bombs: The Top Secret Inside Story of Little Boy and Fat Man* by John Coster-Mullen. The book has details like, "When the breech primers set off the red-colored black powder igniter patches at the rear of the Cordite-filled bags, the resultant explosion propelled the projectile about 52" down the gun and into the target at close to 1,000 fps (feet per second)." His information on the projectile is, "The 16.25" long projectile consisted of nine washer-like, Oralloy (code for Oak Ridge alloy, U-235) rings at the front end with a WC filler plug and thick steel section behind it, assembled in a steel can of 0.0625" wall thickness and weighed about 200-lb."

This is detail like you've never seen before unless you worked in the nuclear arms business. In fact, some have accused Coster-Mullen of letting the cat out of the bag, that he is giving away nuclear secrets. According to Coster-Mullen, he simply gathered information from open sources and then did the calculations to connect the dots. Others have noticed and his diagrams now appear on Wikipedia.

Because of its canon-like mechanism, the U-235 bomb assembly and casing around it were long and slender. The bomb's "Little Boy" name was derived from its shape. It weighed in at just under 10,000 lbs.

At the same time, it became obvious to the researchers that using a reactor to turn uranium into plutonium was easier, cheaper and quicker than the industrial-sized efforts needed to separate U-235 from U-238. Unlike separating alloys, which requires a physical process to collect one atom at a time, plutonium can be separated from other elements using chemical reactions.

This meant that it would be possible to produce many plutonium bombs for every U-235 bomb they constructed, if they could come up with a design to utilize the new element.

The fairly fail-safe Little Boy design wouldn't work for plutonium because of its higher levels of neutron activity. If plutonium were used in the gun-barrel bomb, the pieces would start to fission before they came solidly together. In other words, the early energy released would tend to blow the pieces apart before they became a super critical mass. The result would be, by comparison, a tiny blast.

It was Seth Neddermeyer who pushed the idea for an "implosion" design for a plutonium bomb. The idea of smashing a ball of fissionable material with high explosives was originally proposed by Richard Tolman, but most people considered it too difficult to accomplish. The idea resonated with Neddermeyer as he realized using high explosives to crush a noncritical ball of plutonium into a critical mass would be fast enough to work for plutonium. It was a "sweet" design.

It may have been a sweet design but it was much more difficult to engineer. The upside to accomplishing the plutonium bomb was, according to Coster-Mullen, that the implosion design was 16 times more efficient than the gun-type bomb.

Efficiency in the nuclear weapons world is a very relative term. According to many sources, only two pounds of the plutonium core at Trinity actually fissioned – split into simpler atoms. Out of that mass, only one gram of metal was totally transformed into energy, as in $E=MC^2$. Yet, the explosion was equal to a staggering 42,000,000 pounds of TNT detonating. For perspective, a regular paper clip weighs about one gram.

The famous mathematician John von Neumann added to the design process by suggesting the high explosive material not be a single mass but individually shaped charges – 32 in the final unit with a total weight of about 5,200 pounds. The design was a series of shells or spheres, one encompassing another. The result was a largish ball which gave the bomb its bulbous shape and its name – Fatman.

The explosives could be formed into "lenses" that focused each individual shockwave downward so they blended together into a single wave that would completely envelop the sphere from all sides. If that could be accomplished, the sphere could be uniformly compressed from something the size of a softball down to a blob the size of a golf ball. In addition, von Neumann predicted such a mechanism would be so efficient they could reduce the size of the bomb's core.

Eventually the design called for a sphere of plutonium weighing about 14 pounds to be surrounded by high explosives. To help trigger the chain reaction that would occur at detonation, a smaller sphere composed of beryllium and polonium, a natural neutron generator when the two elements mixed, was placed in the center of the plutonium ball.

According to my contacts in the government, the exact amount of plutonium in the Fatman bomb is still classified. However, the 13 to 14 pound figure has been used for years in all kinds of books and other publications. Coster-Mullen is much more specific in his book. He says the core weighed 13.6 lbs. He goes on to say that President Truman effectively declassified the quantity when he wrote about the Trinity test in his journal saying, "An experiment in the New Mexico desert was startling – to put it mildly. Thirteen pounds of the explosive caused the complete disintegration..."

To make this design work flawlessly, the individually shaped explosive charges had to be perfect. If one or two were flawed, the shockwave wouldn't be evenly distributed over the surface of the core. Such an imbalance might simply blow the core apart making a "dirty" bomb – lots of radioactive fallout but not much bang.

Also, each charge had to be detonated at the same instant or, again, the shockwave would be distorted. When you look at a photo of the plutonium bomb on top of the tower for the Trinity Site test, you can see all the wiring required to connect the charges to the firing source.

The Hanford "B" Reactor, the first reactor built to do nothing but make plutonium, came on line in early 1945. The process soon was known as "breeding" the new element which led to the term "breeder reactors." By summer it had made the plutonium for the bomb tested at Trinity Site and the one dropped over Nagasaki, Japan on August 9, 1945.

Trinity Site Is Needed

Because of doubts about getting the plutonium compression event just right, the decision was made to test the bomb design before trying to use it against Germany or Japan. The test gave the project the opportunity to see if they got it right. At the same time, if there was a problem, they might collect enough data during the test to fix it for the next attempt.

During the spring and summer of 1944, teams led by Ken Bainbridge, the test director, went out looking for the ideal place to test that first bomb. They looked at San Nicolas Island off of the coast of California and an Army desert training base near Rice, California. Sandbars off the coast of southern Texas were also studied. All three of these sites suffered from being too far from Los Alamos.

A site near the Great Sand Dunes National Monument in Colorado and a couple in northwest New Mexico near the lava fields around Grants had terrain and land ownership issues.

Finally, the search narrowed to two sites on the Alamogordo Bombing Range in southern New Mexico. The bombing range was used to train B-17, B-24 and B-29 crews. Its headquarters was what is now Holloman Air Force Base west of Alamogordo, New Mexico. The bombing range was a huge rectangle that extended all the way north to U.S. Highway 380. After the war, that real estate would be the basis for White Sands Missile Range. Eventually the missile range inherited Trinity with the property.

Early on, Holloman and White Sands worked hand in glove. In 1947 Holloman was named the primary site for testing Air Force pilotless air-craft and guided missiles. Eventually the Air Force Missile Development Center was running all kinds of programs from Holloman out onto White Sands.

One site in the middle of the old bombing range was looked at and found to be a long way from Los Alamos and, maybe, too close to Alamogordo and Tularosa. Also, using that site would have cut the bombing range in half, thus negating most of its use.

On the other hand, the northern site on the bombing range was closer to Los Alamos, major highways and a rail line. It was on the north end of the range making the rest of the facility still usable. Downwind there were no sizeable communities.

The selected area has a 3,000-foot wall on the east in the form of the Oscura Mountains. Ground Zero at Trinity is at 4,900 feet above sea level while the high points in the Oscuras are just over 8,000 feet in elevation.

The land generally slopes down to the Rio Grande some 25 miles to the west. Between the mountains and the Rio Grande, all the way south to Las Cruces, is a desolate stretch of desert called the "Jornada del Muerto."

The name originated from when the Spanish owned this part of North

America. They established a route from Mexico City to their northern capital, Santa Fe. Called the "Camino Real" or royal road, it threaded its way through the scrub desert many miles east of the Rio Grande. Most travelers on the road walked, rode horses and hauled things in two-wheeled carts.

The stretch of road from present-day Las Cruces to San Antonio was bone dry with the river tantalizingly close but too far away to use. Also, the Apache, who used the surrounding mountains, would raid the parties traveling on the road.

Because of these difficulties many people died on the route. Usually Jornada del Muerto is translated as "road of death" or "journey of death." However, authors are always trying to come up with new angles, so there are many other translations out there.

This tidbit of local history has been used by many writers in an attempt to create a spot of symbolism for their articles and books about the first atomic bomb test. Many have not been able to resist forcing a connection between the birthplace of the atomic bomb and Spain's "road of death."

What's With The Name?

The most asked question at Trinity Site open houses is "Why is it called Trinity Site?" After the war Groves wondered the same thing. He sent Oppenheimer a letter asking him why he called it Trinity.

Oppenheimer was a bit vague in his reply, saying he didn't remember exactly but he knows he was asked to name the site. He told Groves he remembers reading John Donne poetry at the time and was struck by lines that referred to the idea of resurrection coming through death. For the name, he pulled another Donne line out of the air that seemed to fit his mood, "Batter my heart, three person'd God." From that he moved to "trinity."

Since then a lot of books and news articles have been written and many documentary films made about Trinity Site. Most of the short pieces simply retell this story.

Book authors have a problem with retelling such a simple story. Writing a book requires the author to come up with a new twist to compete with the books already published about Trinity – I should know. Oppenheimer's uncertainty invites speculation. Other writers devote pages to nebulous stories and links to Hinduism, Native American customs, and other Christian stories. It gets rather mystical.

After a while, we in the White Sands Public Affairs Office even got into the act. We reasoned that the bomb test was the culmination of the work done at three sites – Oak Ridge which provided the uranium, Hanford which provided the plutonium, and Los Alamos which designed and built the bomb. They were places wholly invented to build the bomb. It was a trio or triad working together to accomplish the task at hand. Bingo – it was a trinity.

Of course, we knew we were blowing smoke and never seriously advocated the story as the truth either.

By Extension, The Glass Is Trinitite

Another question frequently asked by those delving into the history of the test is, "When did everyone start calling the glass Trinitite?" One of the interesting results of the Trinity test was a crater covered with green glass – glass created from super-heating the desert sand.

The most complete answer I have comes from William Kolb who has done very detailed work on the Trinity story. He is co-author of a book called *Trinitite, 1999, The Atomic Age Mineral* - an updated edition should be out in 2015 - and has analyzed hundreds of pieces of Trinitite. He has even published a detailed radiation map of ground zero.

Also, he is co-author of the very comprehensive *Living With Radiation: The First Hundred Years*. If you want to see all the ways radioactive sources are used in our everyday lives, get a copy of this book.

Kolb put his summary of the name in an email quoted here with his permission:

"*Time Magazine* from September 17, 1945 calls it "glass." The September 24, 1945 issue of *Life* refers to the material as both "fused earth" and "glass." The February 18, 1946 issue of *Time* calls it "glass" and "atomsite." The title of a front page article in the May 17, 1946 *Los Alamos Times* reads, "'Trinitite' Data Sought By Director." The November 1946 piece in *Holiday* calls it "atomsite." In the July 25, 1949 issue of *Time*, it is called "trinitite." The earliest use of the term "Trinitite" I've come across was in an October 22, 1945 letter from Louis Hempelmann, who I believe was in charge of the Los Alamos Health Physics group by then. Before that the material was variously referred to in official correspondence as Trinity Dirt, Crust and Slag, Glass, Fused Glass and TR Glass. Hempelmann doesn't explain the term in his letter, which suggests "Trinitite" was then a familiar word at the Lab."

Jumbo

In August 1944, Groves approved the northern bombing range site as the location for the test. Also, because of the uncertainty of the bomb actually working, Manhattan Project scientists ordered "Jumbo" from Babcock and Wilcox that same month.

The idea was to place the bomb inside Jumbo for the test. If the bomb worked, Jumbo would either be blown to a zillion pieces or vaporized, i.e. turned instantly into gas. If the bomb was a fizzle, Jumbo was designed to contain the detonation of the 5,000 lbs. of high explosives in Fatman and prevent the plutonium from being blown all over the countryside. It might even be recoverable after such an event and reused if Jumbo survived.

Jumbo needed to be 25 feet long, have a 10-foot inside diameter and have rounded or "hemispherical" heads or ends. Initially the Army asked for the walls to be 12 inches thick but soon changed that to 15 inches, just to be safe.

Babcock and Wilcox is an old company founded in 1867 when Stephen Wilcox and George Babcock set about building water tube boilers. By World War I, their boilers were powering a large number of U.S. Navy ships.

At a meeting with company officials, the general requirements for Jumbo, a large cylinder closed at both ends, were laid down. Many people in the past have described its general shape to be like a thermos bottle insert.

Babcock and Wilcox had no idea why they were building such a monstrous container. They looked at the specifications and realized it was bigger and heavier than anything ever constructed before.

According to the company's history of special projects during World War II, they planned to assemble the container in sections and build it up as they went. They first built an inner cylinder or shell using 6.5-inch-thick plate steel. The 15-foot length was "made up of two courses, two plates each, and represented the thickest plates ever rolled up to that time." The heads were composed of several pieces as well to get the appropriate curve.

The shell was then turned on a lathe so the wall thickness was cut down to six inches, which gave them a perfectly smooth surface for the banding process. The next step was to add steel bands around the shell to bring it up to specifications. This was done layer by layer. Each band of steel was a quarter of an inch thick, so 36 layers were added to bring the wall thickness up to the required 15 inches. For added strength each layer of banding was laid so the joints would alternate like the joints in a brick wall.

Because it was many pieces, Jumbo required significant welding to hold it together. Visitors at Trinity Site often look for those welds in the cylinder section of Jumbo that is now on display. Some visitors speculate that Jumbo later failed in 1946 because of the welds. The Babcock and Wilcox analysis of pieces afterwards showed that the welds remained stronger than the plate steel used in construction.

Company officials said in their history that as Jumbo got heavier and heavier, the supporting equipment started to sink into the floor. The final product weighed in at 214 tons.

Once it was complete, they knew of no way to move it out and had no

Since there are no photos of Jumbo being manufactured, we see the first images of the monster on its arrival at the Pope siding just west of Trinity Site. Here workers are preparing to roll it off the railcar onto a platform which they will then jack up and roll a huge trailer under it. Los Alamos photo.

idea where it was going. The Army showed up with a railcar from U.S. Steel that was specially designed for huge weights. U.S. Steel used it to haul gigantic pots of molten steel around their mill.

Jumbo was loaded onto the railcar and a single switching engine was hooked up to move it out of the plant. One account said the engineer wasn't impressed by pulling a single railcar until he hooked up and only managed to spin the engine's wheels. Using lots of sand for traction, he eventually was able to move Jumbo.

Since the railcar was unique, the Army train reportedly traveled at only 20 miles per hour to insure the bearings lasted all the way to New Mexico. Also, they had to take a circuitous route to New Mexico avoiding bridges and tunnels that could not accommodate Jumbo.

Babcock and Wilcox's efforts ended when Jumbo left. It wasn't until after the war they found out what it was used for.

According to Babcock and Wilcox's records, photos were taken periodically of the construction process. An FBI agent was on hand and when the negatives dried he always took them away.

The company was proud of the role it played in the war effort. According to the company's history, they tried several times after the war to retrieve the photos but were unsuccessful.

Buried away somewhere in government archives, like in an Indiana Jones movie, there may be some nice photos of very old equipment being used to assemble a steel pipe with caps at both ends. It is hard to imagine any kind of sensitive military information being contained in the photos. Perhaps the FBI simply lost the photos.

Building The Trinity Site Test Bed

O nce the test area, an 18- by 24-mile rectangle, had been selected on the north end of the bombing range for the plutonium bomb test, Bainbridge went to work planning and building. The first order of business was to select the general area for detonating the bomb. The placement of all instrumentation sites, observation points and base camp would be dictated by that single point or "ground zero."

At GZ, the Army's contractor erected a 100-foot steel tower on which to place the bomb for the test. There are still quite a few people who assume the bomb was somehow dropped from this tower. Nope, it was stationary.

Exploding the bomb at an elevation of 100 feet was done for several reasons. First of all, using such a powerful weapon against an enemy meant exploding it well above the ground. This would allow the shock wave to expand and flatten/damage a much larger area than if the bomb exploded on impact. The 100-foot tower was a scaled simulation of its actual combat use.

Secondly, having the bomb up high provided great views of it from all points. It made for better data collection.

Thirdly, detonation well above the desert floor would greatly reduce the amount of radioactive fallout generated in the blast. It turned out that the crater made at Trinity was only six to nine feet deep – that much material was blasted into the fireball and made radioactive. Resting on the

The 100-foot steel tower at Ground Zero. From the shelter on top, two large coaxial cables stretch out to the left. The copper from these cables may be responsible for the red Trinitite found later. Los Alamos photo.

ground, the blast would have created a crater well over 50 feet deep and hundreds of feet in diameter – an amazing amount of radioactive debris to scatter across New Mexico.

One of the persistent questions visitors ask at Trinity Site open houses is why GZ is where it is. Why not a few miles west, north or south? It is a question we never found an official answer to, as there are no records on the topic at White Sands Missile Range.

However, there is one assumption that can be made about positioning GZ. Because of the known radioactive fallout hazard, all the observation points and base camp would be built upwind based on normal wind conditions. That means these points would be toward the west side of the box with GZ on the east side.

We think that is why GZ sits fairly close to the face of the Oscura Mountains with everything else scattered out to the west on the Jornada del Muerto.

Bainbridge established base camp at the Dave McDonald ranch, about 10 miles southwest of GZ. It is directly upwind of GZ since typical winds are out of the southwest.

The McDonald name causes all kinds of problems for authors and visitors as there were actually three "McDonald" ranches in that area – and they were all related. At base camp, the ranch was actually a partnership between brothers Dave and Ross McDonald. They owned a section or one square mile of land and leased over 20,000 acres (640 acres in a square mile) from New Mexico and the Bureau of Land Management for cattle grazing.

The ranch buildings had been empty since 1942 when the Alamogordo Bombing Range was established. Ranchers and miners were forced to lease their lands to the military for the World War II training range. The Manhattan Project declared the ranch facilities as necessary for the war effort and moved in.

Dave McDonald with his Public Affairs escort Debbie Bingham. Dave showed up at a Trinity open house requesting permission to see his old ranch. Debbie drove the family to the place. White Sands photo.

The McDonald ranch where the plutonium core to the bomb was assembled is only two miles from GZ and once belonged to George McDonald, the third McDonald brother.

It gets trickier still. They were the sons of Tom McDonald who owned a place in Mockingbird Gap, a small pass south of Trinity Site. Tom's ranch was headquartered in a small canyon at the foot of a cliff and was blessed with good water. The missile range calls the place "Ben Site" now.

According to the family, Tom McDonald was ready to resist losing his land to the government at the beginning of 1942. When the Army's Corps of Engineers personnel visited the ranchers to inform them they had to leave, McDonald met them with gun in hand. Family members were present and able to coax the gun from him and get his cooperation.

There is no proof that bombing range personnel held this against McDonald, but during the war the Army loaded his house onto a trailer and hauled it to the range's headquarters area. The bombing range needed buildings and someone decided to take this one.

According to Howard McDonald, Ross' son and Tom's grandson, the house stood on stone footings to keep it level on the slope where it was placed. That made it easy for the military engineers to slide the house off the piers and onto the trailer.

Ross said the family found out about it weeks later from friends who said they saw the house going down the highway through Tularosa, New Mexico. The family investigated and found the house on the bombing range but couldn't get any compensation until they hired a lawyer to confront officials. Remember, the Army was leasing the ranches - it had not purchased them.

Who Were The Schmidts?

Until 1986, the house used for the bomb core assembly was always called the George McDonald place. That was modified when the missile range Public Affairs Office heard from Frances Schmidt. She had seen some of the national publicity generated by the restoration of the house in 1984 and contacted our office.

Through letters written by Frances and her daughter Rosemary Hall, we learned that the McDonald house near GZ was built by Franz Schmidt in 1913.

Franz Schmidt immigrated to the United States through Ellis Island at the age of 17. The young German moved west where he eventually met Ester Holmes of Pearsall, Texas. They were married in 1906.

They moved to New Mexico, still a territory, and established a huge ranch below the Oscura Mountains. Frances, the oldest child, was born in 1908. In 1912, their house burned down while Ester was in town giving birth to their second child, Thomas.

Franz set about building a new four-room adobe house about a mile to the east. The family lived in their barn until the house was complete in 1913. Frances thought they moved in during September.

Because of the previous fire, Franz built this house with an exterior door on each of the four rooms. There was no way anyone was going to be trapped inside.

Frances Schmidt with her mother Ester just after baby Thomas was born. Photo courtesy of Frances Schmidt Hall.

In one letter Frances remembered many details about the house where she spent her childhood. She said the exterior was "pebble dash" and the interior walls were smooth plaster. The kitchen was painted gray, lit by two kerosene lamps and had a Magic Chef range for cooking. The master bedroom was painted pale green and Frances' room was painted blue.

A highlight in the house was the painted border around the top of the living room. Frances said the walls in the living room were a tan or peach color. The scroll work at the top was painted by Mike Walsh, a ranch hand who had come from Chicago seeking relief from tuberculosis.

Since the well water was salty, gutters collected rain flowing off the house's metal roof and diverted it through a box with a charcoal filter into an underground cistern on the west. Also on the west side of the house was a cellar and icehouse. Ice was cut from the water tanks in winter to keep the icehouse cool. The thick door was insulated with sawdust.

To the east of the house they built a bunkhouse. Frank Holmes, Esther's brother, lived there. Also, part of the bunkhouse was used to store groceries and supplies. They ordered large shipments of supplies twice a year so they needed plenty of space for storage.

A barn with attached garage sits just south of the bunkhouse. A large set of corrals is east of the water tanks and barn.

When Frances visited the house when she was in her 90s, she explained that the gates were double-duty gates. You could swing them open to allow horses and cattle in. Also, along the bottom edge, was a short, flap-like area that allowed the sheep to come and go when the main gate was closed. It worked much the way a dog door does.

According to Frances, the family ran about 12,000 sheep and 1,000 cattle. The sheep were divided into six smaller herds, each with a herder and dog. She said the bales of wool were great fun to play on.

Because of health problems, the family sold the ranch and moved to Florida in 1920. To read Schmidt letters, see Apendix B.

Subsequent owners, maybe the McDonalds, built a stone addition on the north side of the house. It held another bedroom and a bathroom. Before the addition, residents used an outhouse on the west side of the home.

Also, the McDonalds added electric lights to the house. Often, visitors to the the house notice the wiring running along the walls and light fixtures hanging from the ceilings and assume the McDonalds had hard power. Not so. The plains of the Jornada del Muerto were not electrified until the missile range started running power lines across them.

Like many ranch families, the McDonalds installed a direct-current system with a wind generator to charge storage batteries. The steel tower on the west side of the house held the windmill for the generator and the batteries were stored in the cellar.

The front of the Schmidt/McDonald ranch house. The door on the left leads into the living room while the other door enters the master bedroom - also the room used in assembling the plutonium core on Friday, July 13. The frame was added by the scientists for hanging a hoist to be used for unloading heavy cargo. Photo by the author.

Working At The Test Site

Construction at Base Camp began in the fall of 1944. Contractors were used to assemble Civilian Conservation Corps (CCC) buildings on site. This strategy of reusing buildings from the 1930s must have been common during and after the war. As the CCC was a quasi-military organization, it made sense that the buildings could be reused by the military. At White Sands Proving Ground, many of the first buildings erected on the main post in 1945 were old CCC structures.

The base camp buildings included barracks, a mess hall, various shops, warehouse, a PX, a dayroom, and a latrine containing showers. Equipment was brought in to generate electricity, pump water and maintain a motor pool.

The first people to occupy Base Camp were military police who arrived on Dec. 30, 1944. In that group was Marvin Davis, a corporal who eventually reached the rank of sergeant.

Davis was born in 1922 in Illinois and was inducted into the Army in 1942. He was trained as a military policeman to include time at the cavalry school learning to ride and care for a horse. He was sent to Los Alamos in April 1943 as part of the mounted police unit providing security at the laboratory.

Marvin Davis and two of the military police horses, Argo and Peergo. Photo courtesy Marvin Davis.

When he arrived on the hill they had no equipment, no horses and no weapons. He said they rode patrol on horses from the old boy's school and carried flashlights and nightsticks. Soon stock was purchased from Las Vegas, New Mexico that gave the young soldiers a taste of "cowboying" as they had to catch these semi-wild horses and try to saddle them. Eventually, better horses were brought in and were part of the group that went to Base Camp.

In 1945, Davis was soon promoted and put in charge of one of the security shifts at Trinity Site. They worked 12-hour shifts – one week of days, one week of nights and one week off. The week off wasn't actually time off but a time when the soldiers pulled other details around the camp.

Mostly the MPs manned a number of checkpoints and towers. Given a little elevation, they could monitor miles and miles of the flat treeless desert with binoculars. One of Davis' jobs was to get his soldiers back and forth from these various checkpoints.

Davis said one day he was changing shifts near Mockingbird Gap. He asked the soldier who had been there for many hours if he had seen anything. The soldier replied he had not, but he was surprised to see a crawdad in such a dry environment.

Davis asked if he had touched it. When the soldier replied in the negative, Davis proceeded to explain what a scorpion was and advised him to be careful. To read excerpts from the Davis letters, see Appendix C.

Apparently scorpions and black widow spiders were a problem in the latrine, especially around the toilet seats. Newcomers had to be advised to be careful when using the facility – check under the seat before sitting.

The 16 horses they brought down to Base Camp were quickly abandoned as working horses. The distances between sites were too great for the horses to be practical. Instead, the horses ended up being used for recreational purposes.

Lieutenant Howard Bush, who was in charge of security and was also the camp commander, worked hard to provide recreational opportunities for his soldiers. They worked in a hot, dry and dirty environment without knowing anything about what was going on. After their work shifts there was very little for personnel to do, so Bush did what he could to boost morale.

Through connections back East he acquired enough real polo gear to equip two teams. It was a nice try but there was no manicured grass field to play on. The uneven terrain proved unworkable for the official wooden balls and small mallets at both Los Alamos and Base Camp. Instead, the men improvised by using a volleyball/soccer ball that easily rolled across the soft sand and brooms that any beginner could use to swat the ball.

In 2000, I received a query from *Polo: Players' Edition Magazine* asking about what they thought was a rumor – soldiers playing polo in the desert during WWII. I gave them the background information and sent some photos. The March 2001 issue carried a nice one-page article about the Trinity Site polo exploits. The only problem was the opening sentence which said, "About 40 miles outside San Antonio, Texas, the U.S. Army had a top-secret site . . . " Some editor must have thought there was only one San Antonio in the United States – he was just 575 miles off the mark.

Military police playing polo at Trinity Site using a volleyball and brooms. Photo courtesy Marvin Davis.

Other recreation included volleyball matches in the evening. In one of Davis' letters to Public Affairs he said, "In the evenings we played a lot of volleyball, we had the net stretched between the latrine and our barracks. I wonder what people would think of volleyball teams with names like Enrico Fermi, George Kistiakowsky and Norris Bradbury on them?"

In another letter, Davis explained that Bush would let trusted soldiers use the Army carbines to hunt deer and antelope. The meat usually ended up in the kitchen as something fresh to supplement whatever the Army was shipping in. He said the antelope was very good but the venison steaks were excellent.

A few of the veterans from Trinity Site who visited years later hinted that some of the cattle that were never rounded up at the beginning of the war ended up as steaks for the men. No one would speak on the record about it although Davis pretty much admits it one of his letters to us.

In addition to hunting, work often brought the soldiers into contact with other desert wildlife. Davis said he retrieved a young hawk from a nest and proceeded to raise it. On patrols they were always killing jack-rabbits and he periodically would bring one back for his hawk. He said, "he (the hawk) could really make the fur fly."

As the bird matured Davis set it free, but it hung around the camp for some time. For a while it would land on the telephone pole that acted as the camp's flagpole. Davis would put a piece of meat out from the mess hall and watch the hawk swoop down to retrieve it.

Felix DePaula, an engineer working at the camp, made more of a pet out of a raven and tamed it enough it would rest on his arm.

DePaula was only 18 when he entered the Army after growing up in New York City. I met him years ago when he visited Trinity Site with a Smithsonian film crew doing oral histories about the Manhattan Project.

He said he was assigned to the Base Camp engineering detail. Since he had no skills, he raised his hand to volunteer when they asked for someone to collect the trash. During his visit, he was able to point out the approximate location of the camp dump to the White Sands archaeologist.

DePaula said he was deathly afraid of snakes and carried a long stick whenever he walked in the desert around camp. He would beat the ground in front of him to scare snakes away.

One day, he and a friend came out of the barracks and saw a snake slither behind some boards stacked against the next building. It was only a bull snake so DePaula took his stick and tried to pry the snake out. He got the end under the snake and tried to lift it out but the stick caught in the boards.

He worked the stick a bit and finally just gave it an energetic jerk. The stick suddenly released upwards and the snake was catapulted right over the building.

He said he gave his friend a look of "oops" and started around the building. Before they got to the end to look out, DePaula said he swore his friend to secrecy.

When they looked out from the corner of the building, they saw a large group of men all looking up in the sky. It turned out the snake flew into the middle of a line of men waiting to get into the mess hall. All they knew was that a snake had dropped on them. Luckily for DePaula, they all thought a hawk had dropped the snake. When he came out, they were looking to see if they could spot the bird flying away.

This photo of some of the support crew at Trinity Site was taken after the test when the use of cameras was permissible. From Carl Rudder's scrap-book.

When DePaula told this story during his visit, he said it was the first time since 1945 he had ever told anyone what had actually happened that day.

Davis, in his letters, mentions capturing a bull snake and carrying it into the recreation hall and watching men scatter "like a bunch of quail." He said several times he thought it was amazing that no one was ever bit by a rattlesnake because they saw a lot of them. He added that whenever he saw one on the roads, he went out of his way to run over it. If he got it just right, it would pop "like a paper bag."

Like most of the soldiers stationed at Trinity, DePaula put in a good word for Lieutenant Bush. He said one time General Groves visited on a Sunday and saw a few men just sitting around relaxing. Groves immediately ordered everyone to work seven days a week. Bush saluted and said "yes sir." Later he told his men he would continue to arrange their schedules so they still received a day off each week.

This is a good example of the difference between a leader and a manager. Groves displayed that typical upper management attitude that hitting the workers with a sledgehammer would get them going. He viewed the men at Trinity Site as mere cogs in the big machine and he wanted all the parts moving to make it look like the work was getting done.

Of course, whether or not the military police, cooks, engineers and

others got a day off here and there made absolutely no difference to when the bomb would be completed and ready for testing. That task rested up at Los Alamos. Bush understood this and knew he would have harder working, more loyal troops by treating them like human beings instead of machines. He was the real leader that day, as those soldiers would have gladly followed him into whatever hellhole he led them. To follow Groves: maybe, maybe not.

Another man sent to Trinity Site was just the opposite of DePaula in that he had a real skill set. In 1945, Carl Rudder of Chattanooga, Tennessee was an experienced power lineman for the Tennessee Valley Authority.

In a letter to the White Sands Public Affairs Office in 1984, Rudder

Carl Rudder, from his scrapbook.

said, "I volunteered for a special assignment under the impression that I was going to Oak Ridge which was near my home. I was inducted on Jan. 26, 1945, passed through four camps, took two days of basic and arrived at Trinity on or about Feb. 17 where I immediately became supervisor of what I named the 'East Jesus and Socorro Light and Water Co."

He went on to say it was a one-man operation and he maintained five generators, three wells and five pumps. He also did all the line work.

You would think that with three wells, the camp and personnel had plenty of water. Not so. Most of the men said the water coming out of the wells was very hard. It was impossible to rinse the soap off your body, and the plumbing at base camp succumbed to calcium buildup in the pipes in just a few weeks.

According to Marvin Davis and others, they eventually resorted to driving into Socorro and hauling potable water in a tanker truck to Trinity for their cooking and personal use.

In addition, Rudder was obviously a trusted man as Bush made him second in command at the camp for most of his stay.

After a short correspondence with Public Affairs, Rudder mailed his photo scrapbook to us and allowed White Sands to copy his pictures. Some have now been published in various histories of the test.

Rudder also provided us with a copy of a letter sent to his wife in December 1945 by a friend of his, Sergeant Loren R. Bourg. Bourg's situation at Base Camp was similar to Rudder's as he turned out to be a one-man operation as well. To read the Rudder and Bourg letters, see Appendix D.

In his letter, the Houma, Louisiana native explained how he received the title of "chief" at Base Camp. He said he was in the fire department in his hometown but was inducted into the Army in November 1942 as a military policeman. Initially he worked at a German prisoner of war camp in Oklahoma. In September 1943, he was reassigned to a fire-fighting unit at Fort Bliss, Texas.

They were supposed to go overseas but instead were shipped to Los Alamos where he was assigned as the "station sergeant." He wrote, "In April of this year (1945) I was sent down here (Base Camp) to take over the fire prevention and fire department. Upon arrival I found I was the fire department period. I was assigned as fire chief and safety officer."

He included a bit of current news when he said, "Carl and I just came in from a fire call. Upon arrival at the scene, we found that it was an overheated coal heater. The soot burnt out of the pipe causing the pipe to turn white hot."

Bourg finished his letter with, "This is my fourth Christmas to be celebrated in an Army post. Every Christmas day so far, I had to work. This Christmas Eve night I will be in charge of quarters. That means no sleep. So Christmas Day I will be asleep, I hope." He added a postscript saying,

"This is the first time I was ever real homesick on Christmas."

In January 1945, Dave Rudolph, a young inventory clerk, was sent to Trinity from Los Alamos as the aide to the post engineer, Capt. Samuel Davalos. Later he said, "Life on The Hill was isolated; life at Trinity was penal."

What happened to Rudder and Bourg was fairly common for soldiers serving at Trinity Site. Brand new personnel like Rudder, more experienced folks like Bourg, and a few veterans who had actually experienced combat ended up in the middle of the desert without a clue as to why they were really there. Some of them had signed on expecting to go out and contribute to the war effort.

Working in the desert in secret conditions didn't seem like much of a contribution. Many were frustrated by their initial time at Trinity. That, of course, changed on July 16, 1945 when they saw the test – they joined a very select fraternity of men and women who made a unique contribution.

To Collect Test Data

You test something new to see if it works as advertised and collect as much information during the test as possible. If it doesn't work, that data can help fix it afterward.

Since the test at Trinity was a cutting-edge, first-ever item, they needed to not only find out if it worked, but how it matched their theories and calculations, and what its effects were.

Mostly there were very few off-the-shelf instruments that could be used to collect this data. The scientists and engineers, under the leadership of physicist Robert Wilson, had to be ingenious in developing new instruments or modifying common devices to get the data they wanted. Also, they had to invent ways to protect instruments so they would survive the radiation and blast effects.

Wilson went on to oversee building the National Accelerator Laboratory which is frequently called "Fermilab." Wilson was its first director.

In many ways the collection of data became a series of "experiments" in itself, since this had never been done before. This reality is reflected in the title of the brochure written by Thomas Merlin of Human Systems Research for White Sands Missile Range concerning the instrumentation. It is called *The Trinity Experiments*.

The size of the workforce at Trinity Site in the months leading up to the test is a testament to this need to collect data. Soldiers, scientists and engineers spent weeks laying out communication lines to shelters, bunkers and mounts for the hundreds of instruments and devices scattered around the test bed.

During this buildup of test equipment and experiments, a committee was established to review and approve or reject proposals. This was necessary because Bainbridge was quickly flooded with requests by scientists wanting to collect all sorts of information. As the test date approached, they simply shut off all requests because they couldn't deal with them all.

One scientist told me that some of them conducted a few experiments on their own. One group was interested in biological effects of the blast. There was no time to put together any kind of complex task, so the experimenter simply acquired some lab rats and tied them by their tails to wiring cross arms at various distances from GZ. Because of safety restrictions, he had to place the rats too early in the day and was not allowed back into the area. One of the security people on night patrol noted that the rats all died before the explosion. They figured it was just too much time in the heat without shade or water.

Contractors like Brown Construction out of Albuquerque did much of the heavy work. Ted Brown, founder of Brown Construction, said in an Associated Press story in August 2000, that his company built 45 miles of roads, shelters and several towers to include the one on which the bomb was placed. He said the operation was so secret he signed a blank contract with the dollar amounts to be filled in later.

At 10,000 yards from GZ at points south, west and north of the tower, Brown constructed shelters with concrete roofs. These shelters housed a few men with instruments and cameras. These observers were the closest people to GZ at the time of the explosion.

The shelter at the south point was the operation's nerve center. Robert

The South 10,000 yard bunker. Note all the communications lines feeding out of the shelter. This was the control bunker for the test. Los Alamos photo.

Oppenheimer watched from here, the countdown originated from here, and the signals sent to trigger the instruments and the gadget started here.

Although these shelters are given direction names, they do not sit on points directly south, west or north from GZ.

Also, a number of small instrumentation bunkers were constructed closer to GZ. For instance, one bunker visitors see as they drive into the site during open houses is only 800 yards from GZ. That bunker was originally built to protect Fastax cameras.

According to Berlyn Brixner, Los Alamos photographer, he had to change plans for some of these cameras. Tests determined that cameras close to GZ, like the ones at the west 800-yard bunker, would be exposed to high levels of radiation and the film would never survive.

Before the test, the cameras were moved to a sled outside the bunker. Brixner and his team fabricated lead boxes to protect the cameras. The boxes were mounted on the sled that was placed next to the 800-yard bunker. The cameras were pointed straight up through windows made of leaded glass. Mirrors were positioned over the cameras and angled so each camera was focused on the tower.

After the test, the crews used the thousand-foot cable attached to the sled to pull it back to their position. This eliminated any unnecessary exposure to the high levels of radiation in the immediate GZ area right after the explosion.

Some of the cameras at North 10,000. The large camera is a Mitchell 35mm movie camera - the same kind of camera used to shoot Hollywood movies at the time. Los Alamos photo.

When you stand in the west 800-yard bunker, you can look out through pipes that were planned viewing ports in the east wall and see GZ. There is also a pipe on the south wall that is angled to the southeast. It looks like this viewing port was built to provide a view of the 100-ton TNT test site south of GZ. A camera mounted in the bunker would have been able to safely record the May 7 dry run. No one seems to know if it was used or not.

Cameras alone varied from simple pinhole boxes to measure gamma radiation to 37 motion picture cameras. Fastax cameras running at 1,000 frames per second captured those images of the initial stages of the explosion. Mitchell 35mm cameras were used to track the rise of the mushroom cloud and track it as it moved northeast.

Some of the instruments like cameras and seismographs required power to operate. Others like blast gauges and crusher boxes were simply set up beforehand and retrieved when convenient.

Miles of communication and power cable were strung or buried all over the test bed. Some of the poles and cross arms for these lines are still standing today.

Moisture was an issue for the wiring laid on the ground or buried. To protect their work, the crews went into town and purchased as much garden hose as they could get. They then ran the wire through the hose to keep the water out.

As in any complex undertaking, not everything went right. For instance, Robert Walker worked to protect cables going to dozens of gauges he had in the field, but still ended up with no data from the blast. Given that fact, he said he made a big mistake during the test because he paid so much attention to his equipment, he missed seeing the first part of the explosion.

On the night of the test, personnel stationed at various bunkers didn't receive much information about the rain delay from 4 to 5:30 a.m. for the detonation. On one of his visits to Trinity Site, Brixner told me he knew there was a delay at 4 a.m. but had no idea what the new test time was.

Brixner was on top of the North 10,000-yard bunker and was one of the few people allowed to watch the test from outside a bunker that close in. He was manning a 35mm Mitchell motion picture camera mounted in a machine gun turret that required him to track the fireball and cloud. The camera was equipped with a 75mm lens and was running at 24 frames per second.

He said he never heard when the new detonation time was, but some seconds before the blast his camera was powered up and he knew it was time to go to work. The camera was switched on by the automatic-sequencing system located in the South 10,000-yard bunker. When the switch was thrown to start the process, cameras and other instruments sprang to life, flares were ignited, and the bomb was triggered at a precise moment in the sequence.

Also at Brixner's position were two other Mitchell cameras – fixed in position. One was equipped with a 450mm lens for a much closer view of the explosion. It was running at over 100 frames per second to provide a slow-motion view. The other camera had a 610mm lens and was focused on the two barrage balloons just to the west of the tower. It was running at almost 120 frames per second.

The videos from these three cameras is readily available for viewing on line from numerous sources.

With those dozens of cameras scattered around the test site, most visitors are surprised there are no decent color movies of the Trinity test. If you do see some color video claiming to be from the Trinity test, you know it is fake or from some other test. Brixner said there were numerous cameras at the site loaded with color film but none of it turned out.

In a 1985 letter to Brigadier General Niles Fulwyler, then commander of White Sands, Brixner said two cameras at his location "didn't run, my other cameras recorded all phases of the explosion." He added that the stop-action photos of the early moments of the test everyone uses are "enlargements from my 35mm movie films."

In those still photographs from the first few seconds of the explosion, there are two little clouds of smoke and two vertical lines that are to the right of the growing fireball. These are the remains of the two barrage balloons and the steel cables anchoring them.

The author, left, interviewing Berlyn Brixner at the Trinity Site open house on April 7, 1990. WSMR photo.

First of all, barrage balloons were used in World War II for defense against German bombers. Around London, helium filled balloons would be left floating in the sky with steel cables hanging down from them. They would be anchored to the ground so they would stay in place. The idea was that attacking aircraft might get entangled in the net of cables and be disabled and crash. One report said they also brought down many of the German V-1 flying bombs.

In 1945, the balloons were readily available and Los Alamos scientists thought to float some instumentation near the test tower to capture data like the neutron flux at the beginning of the explosion. One problem, being only a few hundred feet from the tower, the incredible flash of radiation at the very beginning vaporized the balloons and their cables – they were turned to smoke long before the fireball arrived.

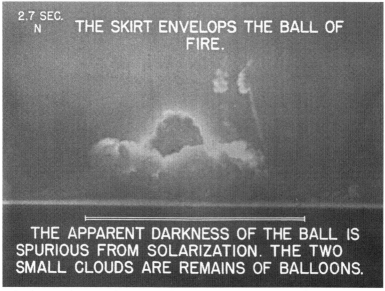

The Los Alamos labelling on this photo, taken less than three seconds after detonation, pretty much tells the story of the balloons and the cables. They are already smoke. Los Alamos photo.

The same color void exists for still images of the Trinity test. There is only one decent color photograph of the explosion and it didn't come from the designated official cameras. That one photo was taken rather unofficially by Jack Aeby. He wasn't a photographer and described himself as a jack-of-all-trades for the Health Physics Group. He had nothing to do on test morning so his boss, Emilio Segre, gave him a camera and sent him out into the dark near base camp to take pictures.

He said he sat on a straight-backed chair with the back in front of him so he could prop his arms and the camera on the back. Thinking the test might be a dud, he started with the camera's aperture wide open to catch whatever spark or puff might be seen from 10 miles away. The aperture is like the pupil of the eye and can be very wide to let in lots of light at night or just a pinpoint in the bright sunlight.

In a visit to Trinity Site decades after the test, Aeby said, "When it became apparent that it was a successful detonation, I released the shutter and cranked the aperture down and shot three in rapid succession. The middle one was about the right exposure. I'd have taken more, except I ran out of film."

Jack Aeby during a return visit to Trinity Site in 2005. WSMR photo.

That iconic color mushroom cloud image has been used worldwide for decades. As the only color photo no one has had much choice. It is not a particularly good picture so many editors opt instead to use one of the crisp black and white pictures captured by Brixner.

When he was interviewed at White Sands, Aeby said he has seen the photo so many times, he sometimes wished he could get a nickel for every T-shirt, cap, mug, newspaper or magazine story using it. He laughed and said the only payment he ever received was $200 from *Life* magazine after his wife got after them.

Over the years, the White Sands Public Affairs Office was often asked to look at some nice color photographs or video of a mushroom cloud and verify it was from the Trinity test. Most of the time it was a no-brainer response since it was in color. Also, a lot of the presented material was shot in broad daylight with the sun clearly high in the sky – it is easy to tell by examining the shadows. It certainly wasn't shot 35 minutes before sunrise.

The 100-Ton Calibration Test

On May 7, 1945, Los Alamos conducted a calibration test and dry run at Trinity Site. A 20-foot wooden platform was constructed southeast of the GZ tower. Wooden crates filled with TNT was delivered to the Pope railroad siding by freight car and trucked to GZ. A total of 100 tons of TNT was stacked on the platform.

Gaps were left in the stack so plastic tubing could be snaked through

A look down on the men stacking the boxes of TNT for the 100-ton explosion. Note that instead of making a square shape, they are stacking to make a more circular formation. There are cables running through the stack that are anchored in vertical boards on the ends to help hold the boxes firmly together until detonation. Los Alamos photo.

the explosives. The tubing was filled with a radioactive slurry from a reactor at Hanford.

The test was used to calibrate many of the instruments with a known quantity of explosives. Since then, we have seen the yield of nuclear explosions equated to the explosive force of so many tons of TNT.

The test also acted as a dress rehearsal for the real deal with a countdown and automatic switching to activate some of the instruments.

Finally, measuring radiation levels from the slurry in and around the crater afterwards gave scientists some hint at what to expect during the real test. They even drove one of the lead-lined tanks into the small crater – about five feet deep and 30 feet across – to retrieve soil samples just as they would for the real test.

Jumbo's Final Role

Jumbo arrived by train from Ohio in early June. It was unloaded from the special railroad car at Pope siding about 25 miles west of the test site. It was rolled onto a heavy structure of steel girders that was then jacked up so a special trailer equipped with 64 wheels could be pushed under it.

Workers pose in front of Jumbo on its special trailer. Los Alamos photo.

Bulldozers were used to pull and push the trailer on a specially constructed road to GZ. By the time it arrived, the scientists had already decided not to use Jumbo. One reason was they were confident the test would work and Jumbo was irrelevant. Also, if they decided to use it and the bomb was successful, the 214 tons of steel would interfere with collecting data during those first few milliseconds of the explosion. Thirdly, by not using Jumbo, they eliminated spraying 214 tons of activated steel (made radioactive by neutron bombardment) into the atmosphere to become fallout.

Instead, they hauled Jumbo to a spot about 800 yards west of GZ. There, not until after Jumbo arrived, work crews erected a heavy-duty tower to hang Jumbo from.

A photo of it a few feet off the ground has led many to assume it was hanging during the test. For the test, Jumbo was lowered onto a concrete pad with a dimple in it to accommodate the curved end of Jumbo. Thus it was standing upright for the test, resting between the legs of the tower.

The explosion did not damage Jumbo. However, the blast crumpled the steel tower standing around Jumbo and scoured the earth away from some of the tower's foundations. What happened to the tower was detailed by Groves in his report to the Pentagon on the strength of the explosion.

On April 16, 1946 at 11:30 a.m. with Jumbo still standing on end, eight 500-pound bombs were exploded inside it. It was supposedly done to dispose of the bombs. Afterward the Army officers sounded contrite, but it is easy to imagine a bunch of guys sitting around wondering what would happen if they put the bombs in Jumbo – "Gee whiz, it'll be sharp!"

According to First Lieutenant Richard Blackburn who filed a report afterwards with Sandia Base, "The foundation was pulverized and scattered over a large area. Both ends were torn off 'Jumbo' and fragments were thrown as far as three-quarters of one mile. A piece, estimated to weigh over fifteen tons, landed 750 feet from the site."

The report was sent to Lieutenant Colonel A.J. Frolich, the commander of Sandia. Frolich, in turn, sent a memo up the chain of command saying he approved Blackburn's request to dispose of the eight bombs in Jumbo because "the charge was less than the total supposed to be set off in 'Jumbo,' I approved . . ." He added, "I regret Jumbo was destroyed, but wish to state that all responsibility for the decision is the undersigned."

Jumbo in its final position before the test - 800 yards from GZ. Los Alamos photo.

The military had to sound a bit regretful because they acted without consulting scientists at Los Alamos and those folks were upset when they heard the news. Los Alamos did all the work to design this crazy container based on nothing but theoretical calculations. Then they paid very good money to have it built and shipped to New Mexico. What was aggravating was they got no science, no data from the event. Afterward they were still left wondering if their design was worth the time and effort or not.

Frolich also added that since Jumbo was destroyed it could be salvaged to alleviate "the present shortage of steel." However, nothing was done with Jumbo for years. It rested partially buried on its side until someone salvaged the steel bands off of it. The question to answer is when did the bands disappear?

Military personnel from the missile range often hunted pronghorn on the plains on the north end of White Sands. One of those soldiers, Frank Conway, let Public Affairs copy a photo he had of Jumbo taken in the early

1950s. The hunters are posed in front of Jumbo and the nine inches of banding are still there.

The ruin of Jumbo in the early 50s. The steel bands are intact and the inner shell has jagged edges where the steel failed. Photo courtesy Frank Conway.

As best as I can determine, the bands disappeared before 1960. My suspicion is they were removed as scrap. The Jumbo tower also disappeared at some point in the 50s. I assume the bands and the steel from the tower made a sizable scrap pile.

Of course, this has implications for the current weight of Jumbo. With the rounded ends or caps gone and nine inches of steel bands AWOL as well, Jumbo is a mere shadow of its former self. Using some simple math and a generic weight for a cubic foot of steel, I estimate the Jumbo shell now weighs between 50 and 55 tons – 110,000 pounds max. That is tons lighter than an Abrams tank. I suspect most visitors have no idea it is a fraction of the original and they assume it is much heavier than it really is.

In today's world, Jumbo's weight would be just a footnote. Those huge mining trucks that move ore are capable of carrying loads of 300 to 400 tons.

It may have been that false perception of Jumbo's extreme weight that saved it from being given away. Preston Pond, president of the Socorro County Chamber of Commerce, wrote a letter on June 27, 1960 to Captain Norman Banda, Commander of Stallion Site on White Sands Missile

Range, requesting Jumbo be donated to Socorro to create a historical monument to that first test. He said, "If the cylinder were donated for that purpose, we plan to place it in a tourist park on both U.S. Highways 85 and 60, with a large sign on the highway to inform travelers of its historic significance."

He also said, "Inasmuch as Trinity Site is open to the public only one day a year..." Missile range records are spotty but this shows there were regular public visits to the site before 1960.

On July 1, 1960, Captain Banda sent a memo to the missile range's troop commander saying, "Request the cylinder be released to be used in the monument, and that the Post Engineers assist in its movement to the site in So-

corro." Later in July, Lieutenant Colonel Donald Jones, Chief of Logistics at White Sands, sent a letter to the Atomic Energy Commission. He told the commission Jumbo was not on the missile range's property book. He assumed it was part of the Trinity test and asked the commission to check their records and donate it to Socorro if possible.

Eventually, according to press

All that is left of Jumbo today is the inner shell. It rests in the parking lot for all to see. Author's photo.

reports, Jumbo would be donated to Socorro if the city could get it moved. Dale Green, who worked for the Post Engineers at Stallion in 1960, said he always heard Jumbo was too heavy to be hauled over the Rio Grande highway bridge at San Antonio. That is why it is still on White Sands.

If the planners were thinking Jumbo still weighed close to 180 tons, they didn't have a trailer that could handle or distribute the load enough to make it legal on the highway or meet the bridge's load capacity.

Jumbo rested peacefully in the sand until 1979 when Public Affairs convinced the White Sands command group to move it up to the Trinity Site parking area so visitors could see it. Visitors were always asking about it and wondering if they could wander out into the desert to see it.

Instead of trying to lift and carry it to its new location, the engineers at Stallion Range Center used a little ancient Egyptian technology sped up by a bulldozer. They bulldozed a ramp down below Jumbo. This allowed them to back a flatbed trailer down the ramp so the bed was level with Jumbo. Then they simply rolled Jumbo onto the trailer using the bulldozer.

At the designated resting site in the parking lot, another ramp was dug. With the help of the dozer, the truck hauled Jumbo to the spot and backed down the ramp. The engineers then rolled Jumbo off to its final resting spot.

Visitors now walk right past it as they make the walk down to GZ. Kids love trying to run up the inside curve of Jumbo. There is a large amount of gouging and damage on the inside at one end of the tube. This is the end that was on the ground in 1946 when the 500-pound bombs were placed inside it.

Bomb Preparation

At first Los Alamos officials were planning for a test on July 4 – the ultimate firecracker. However, more testing at Los Alamos was required, so they pushed the test to the middle of July. Once the scientists and engineers deemed it ready, the whole process fell into the hands of the weather forecasters.

July and August in New Mexico are known as the monsoon months as the state gets most of its moisture in those two months. Thunderstorms build as the summer heat pushes moist air up the slopes of the many mountain ranges. The storms drift off over valleys and plains bringing violent winds, heavy rains and hail.

Long-range forecasts predicted a break in this pattern around July 16. It became a target for the men to get everything done.

On Thursday, July 12, the two pieces of the plutonium core were transported to the Schmidt/McDonald ranch house in an ordinary Army sedan. The main part of the bomb with its thousands of pounds of high explosives followed on Friday, July 13.

The ranch house was perfect because it was a good solid structure and only two miles from GZ. The men turned the master bedroom into a clean room. They nailed plastic over the windows to try and seal it. They taped the edges and the various joints in the room to keep dust out. They even chalked a warning on the front door telling all who entered to wipe their feet.

The plutonium arrived at the ranch house about 6 p.m. and was delivered to the clean room by Sergeant Herbert Lehr. There is a famous photo of Lehr carrying a box with rubber bumpers through the door of the ranch house.

Herb Lehr taking the plutonium hemispheres into the assembly room at the Schmidt/McDonald ranch house. The chalked message on the door reads, "Please use other doors - keep this room clean." Los Alamos photo.

In the photo there is a hat hanging on the wall. According to an interview in 1983 with the Department of Energy historian, Dr. Robert Bacher said that was his hat. He went on to say he didn't remember being there for the plutonium delivery, but recognizing his hat made him believe he was there. Bacher was head of the Gadget Division at Los Alamos.

Also, Bacher said the idea in the ranch house was to use one of their special kits to assemble the core. Some of these kits with tools and parts were already on their way to the tiny Pacific island of Tinian where scientists would assemble the bombs for delivery to Japan. Testing the tool kits was essential to ensure their adequacy for the job a few weeks later.

Dr. Phil Morrison accompanied the plutonium and carried two initiators in his pocket. Lehr referred to the initiators as "urchins." Both he and Dr. Boyce McDaniel later related how Morrison played a game with the two urchins, asking people to guess which one was the real one and which one was the dummy.

People were flabbergasted as he freely mixed the two, making it impossible to visually tell them apart. They were worried because the initiator was made to naturally eject neutrons at detonation to help start the chain reaction in the plutonium. To put the wrong one in the core could have been a major blunder.

The initiator was made of polonium and beryllium. At the bomb's very center, when the two were crushed together, alpha particles released by the polonium would trigger an in-kind release of neutrons from the beryllium into the plutonium that surrounded it. This would happen just as the plutonium was being crushed into a critical mass and was all that was needed to jump-start the chain reaction.

What many people didn't realize was that the radioactivity of the initiator made it warm to the touch while the dummy would be ambient temperature. Morrison had no trouble telling which was which.

The plutonium hemispheres and the initiator spent the night in the ranch house. The next morning the pit assembly crew gathered to put it together.

McDaniel said Dr. Marshall Holloway and Dr. Raemer Schreiber did most of the work. Lehr said in an interview that McDaniel and Schreiber put it together. They had to smooth some of the surfaces of the metals, but basically they simply placed the initiator into the hollowed out area in the plutonium hemispheres and put the plutonium pieces together.

Earlier I described the core as the size of a softball. Lehr described it as being the size of a baseball. Others described it as the size of a grapefruit. In his book, Coster-Mullen doesn't compare the core size to anything else. He simply states it was 3.62 inches in diameter. When you look up a list of balls used in sports, the croquet ball and softball are the closest in size. Using fruit seems totally inadequate as individual pieces of any fruit can vary greatly in size. Whatever you use for comparison, it was a remarkably small package to be able to destroy a city.

At the ranch house, the ball was then placed into a short column of uranium nine inches tall and five inches in diameter. In other words, the ball of plutonium was placed into the center of a "plug" of uranium shaped like a large can. This is a step often missed by reporters.

Already inside the bomb apparatus at GZ was a larger sphere of uranium with a hole drilled in it to accept the plutonium/uranium package or plug. This larger sphere surrounded the plutonium to keep the chain reaction going for a few billionths of a second longer before the core blew itself apart. The longer the chain reaction ran, the bigger the blast.

One of the photos taken at the ranch house shows two men carrying a box between them on a litter with a car nearby. This photo is often misidentified as showing the plutonium being taken from the car to the house. According to Lehr and others, the litter photo was taken as Lehr and Harry Daghlian were moving the assembled core and plug to the car for its trip to GZ on the 13th.

Just a few weeks later, the same Harry Daghlian was conducting critical assembly tests at Los Alamos when he dropped a tamper block on a plutonium core. The assembly went critical. Daghlian understood the danger and immediately brushed the tamper aside. He and a guard in the room both reported a blue flash of light. Daghlian's calculated dose was about 510 Rems.

The accident was on Aug. 21, 1945. Daghlian died on Sept. 25.

Lehr and Daghlian carry the assembled plutonium/uranium plug to an Army sedan for transport to GZ two miles away. It took two men to safely handle the heavy plug. Los Alamos photo.

So how much did the plug weigh if it took two men to safely carry it? In his interview at Trinity Site in 2005, Lehr estimated the package weighed about 40 pounds.

That is considerably heavier than the 14-pound core and would explain two men carrying the package with a litter. I decided to doublecheck the weight in *The Making Of The Atomic Bomb* by Richard Rhodes which is considered by many to be the bible for the Manhattan Project. He didn't give a weight for the total package. Instead, he reported that the scientists laid out the parts on a table and they included the initiator, two plutonium hemispheres and "the cylindrical 80-pound plug of tamper."

OK, that is easy to add together for a total weight of about 95 lbs. – a significant difference from 40 lbs.

Next I looked into Coster-Mullen's book and he reported the package weighed about 120 lbs. OK, another large discrepancy, but we are definitely getting to weights that explain why two men were required to move the plug to the car for transport. But which one is correct?

The only way to tell, since Los Alamos isn't going to comment, is to do the math. It was easy to find the densities of both plutonium and uranium and to calculate the volume of the plug. Run the formulas and the answer turns out to be just over 120 lbs. Definitely a two-man job.

Under the tower at GZ, a tent had been erected to protect the bomb mechanism that rested between the tower's four legs. At this stage "Friday the 13th" bad luck almost struck the operation. As the scientists went to lower the plutonium/uranium plug into the center of the bomb, it jammed. It didn't fit.

As they scratched their heads and each took a turn at peering into the opening to see what was the matter, the temperatures of the cylinder and the bomb itself equalized. Finally, much to their relief, the cylinder slid home into the center of the bomb.

After they buttoned up the bomb, they assembled everything to the point of installing the detonators. They took the rest of the day off.

On Saturday, July 14, the crew removed the tent at 8 a.m. and hoisted the bomb to the corrugated steel shelter at the top of the tower. This was

The bomb on top of the 100-foot tower at GZ with Norris Bradbury looking on. Note all the wiring necessary to trigger the 32 lenses of high explosives surrounding the plutonium core. Bradbury would go on to succeed Oppenheimer as director of Los Alamos. Los Alamos photo.

a slow process. The Department of Energy timeline from 1983 states the bomb traveled about one foot per minute.

The slow ascent gave nervous personnel a chance to stack mattresses under it as it went up. This effort is often assumed to be the result of concern that the bomb might explode if it was dropped. According to Norris Bradbury, they piled up the padding because they were afraid of damaging the bomb if it dropped.

The bomb made it to the top safely and by 5 p.m. was completely assembled and ready to go. At that point the test site was evacuated and only essential personnel were allowed in.

One of the essential people was Boyce McDaniel. He climbed the tower every four hours until early in the morning on July 16, in order to pull a long manganese wire out of the bomb and replace it with a new one. A tiny gap had been left so this could be accomplished.

The wire was a clever way to measure neutron activity in the core of the bomb. Neutrons activated the manganese and made some of its atoms radioactive. The more neutrons, the more radioactive the wire would be. The measurements proved steady throughout the night.

People gathered at various points throughout the night and early morning of July 16 to watch the test, perform assigned duties, and be ready if needed. The closest personnel were at the shelters 10,000 yards south, west and north of GZ.

Sometimes visitors ask why there was no east bunker. The answer is simple: prevailing winds would have carried the radioactive fallout in that direction.

That hasn't stopped writers from playing with the idea. In 1981, science fiction writer David Houston published *Tales of Tomorrow – Invaders at Ground Zero*. The novel was written as a public disclosure and claims there really was an east shelter manned by scientists and medical personnel. What happened there was supposedly buried in secrecy by the government.

The story line was that an alien spacecraft crashed near the site just a day or so before the test. The scientists responded and found a dying creature. Unknown to them was the fact the alien was dying because he was infected with a virus-like entity that could jump from one species to another and control the individual's actions. These microbes possessed a "group intelligence" and could communicate with each other.

Just as the alien died, the virus jumped to one of the humans. As the virus tried to take control, it killed its human host and jumped to another and then another, gaining more control each time. In the end, the humans figured it out, but were dropping like flies. Finally, a man and woman were infected and realized they were doomed. To prevent further spread, they isolated themselves from the few humans left.

In a heroic act, they then walked to GZ and sat under the tower. They heard the countdown knowing the explosion would not only kill them but kill the virus as well. They saved us all.

The Explosion

Most personnel watched the test from base camp safe from the explosion and any aliens who might come by. In fact, there were a couple of hundred people there to include the support soldiers like Felix DePaula and Carl Rudder. The more famous included Maj. Gen. Leslie Groves, Enrico Fermi, Vannevar Bush, Phil Morrison, I.I. Rabi, James Conant, Victor Weisskopf, Emilio Segre, and Ken Greisen.

At the South 10,000 yard bunker, in addition to Oppenheimer and Bainbridge, there were Sam Allison, Frank Oppeheimer, Lt. Howard Bush, Joe McKibben, Donald Hornig, Ernest Titterton, Louis Hempelman, George Kistiakowsky, and Brig. Gen. Thomas Farrell.

A number of VIPs including Edward Teller, Hans Bethe, Ernest Lawrence, Richard Feynman, James Chadwick and Robert Serber were taken in buses to their own viewing area. Also in this group was Klaus Fuchs, the German-born British physicist who delivered atomic bomb secrets to the Soviet Union. Finally, New York Times reporter Bill Laurence also watched from there.

They were dropped at a small hill south of U.S. Highway 380 and about 20 miles northwest of GZ. The hill is variously called Campania, Compana, and Compagna Hill by reporters and Manhattan personnel.

On current maps, Cerro de la Compana is a hill at the north end of a cluster of hills just northwest of the missile range's Stallion Range Center. According to former missile range archeologist Bob Burton, the named hill does not provide an unobstructed view of GZ. Other ridges get in the way. Red Butte, however, which is just southeast of Cerro de la Campana, gives a great open view out toward Trinity Site. In surveying Red Butte, Burton identified some old disturbed ground that might date to the viewing site in 1945.

The witnesses had no facilities and tended to not know much about where they were in the local landscape. One told me he arrived on a bus in the middle of the night and the bus left before the sun rose. He never saw anything too clearly.

Others, such as military police, medical personnel and soldiers, were on the perimeter of the test area providing security and monitoring radiation levels after the blast. For instance, Sergeant Marvin Davis escorted a technician with a Geiger counter as they traveled north along the west boundary.

Other soldiers and technicians with radiation monitors were stationed north along U.S. Highway 380 and northeast, near Carrizozo, waiting to see if it was necessary to evacuate the towns or ranches downwind from the test.

Some people didn't get invited but took it upon themselves to find a viewing spot. Harold Argo described himself as a junior guy "who punched a calculator." He wanted to see the test so he studied topographic maps of the area and selected Chupadera Peak, just south of Socorro and west of the highway. He said he could see the site with binoculars but was obviously way too far away to hear the loudspeaker announcements. He didn't realize the shot was delayed because of weather.

At 5:25 he decided to leave. He threw his blanket over his shoulder, took 10 steps down the hill, and suddenly everything lit up.

Personnel out in the open such as Brixner at the 10,000 yard shelters, at base camp and on Compania Hill, were all issued a piece of welder's glass mounted in a piece of cardboard. They were told to look away from the tower at detonation; after the first few seconds, they could hold their piece of dark glass up to their eyes and look at the explosion through it.

That is an interesting bit of planning and precaution given that some accounts of the test portray the scientists as not knowing what they were doing. In reality, they had a very good idea of what was going to happen.

As the night progressed, thunderstorms rolled through the area. The test was scheduled for 4 a.m. but was delayed because of the storms. After discussions with the weather forecaster, Oppenheimer and Groves decided to delay until 5:30 instead of waiting for another day.

There were two reasons for not waiting a whole day. One, the meteorologist thought the storms might clear out by 5:30. (He proved right.) Two, with the rain, winds and electrical strikes, every delay increased the chances of serious problems with the bomb and all the associated equipment.

Given all the histories written since 1945, one would think it rained buckets that night. I've asked many people who watched from base camp if it was muddy when they laid down on the ground at 5:25. They have all said "no."

For his family, Stanley Hall wrote about his experiences at Los Alamos during the war and his time at Trinity Site. At GZ he worked on a device to measure neutrons and transmit that data to a remote underground bunker. The information was to be used for analysis if the bomb failed.

About the rain at base camp he wrote: "Hollywood movies portraying the event usually show a heavy downpour the night of the test, but all I remember is an occasional drizzle. Base Camp was really on the old McDonald Ranch where there was a ranch "tank" (that's what it is called) made by a bulldozer. We spent all night on the slope or side of the tank and certainly would not have done that in a heavy rain."

So apparently it didn't rain at base camp. Richard Watts, in his recollection of the night, said Oppenheimer and Groves would go out into the rain at the South 10,000-yard shelter and dodge puddles on the asphalt as they discussed their weather decision. They must have had at least a light shower there.

Based on these folks' experiences, it appears there were typical New Mexico thunderstorms that night. After midnight, many of the storms may have lost their ferocity and only managed to produce light rains to drizzles.

At 5:30 the bomb was triggered. It was immediately obvious that it worked, maybe beyond their wildest expectations.

There were hundreds of eyewitnesses and they generally agree on the sequence of events. However, like most events reported by individual humans, they disagree on some of the details. Edwin McMillian watched from Compania Hill and said in his memo on July 19, "None of my estimates of times or magnitudes can be considered very accurate, as I have found by comparison with others a wide variation, illustrating the difficulty of personal judgment without instruments."

The first thing they all experienced was an incredible flash of white light. Most describe it as many times brighter than the noonday sun. At the same time they felt heat on their skin.

McMillian reported, "I was watching the shot through a piece of dark glass such as is used in welders' helmets. An exceedingly bright light appeared and expanded very rapidly. I was aware of a sensation of heat on my face and hands, which lasted about a second. After about two seconds, I took the glass away. The sky and surrounding landscape were brightly

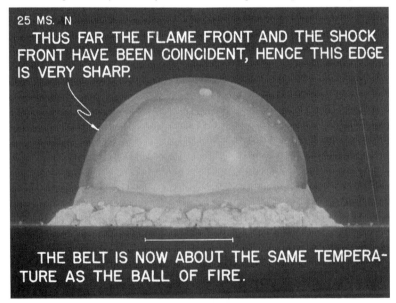

25 MS. N
THUS FAR THE FLAME FRONT AND THE SHOCK FRONT HAVE BEEN COINCIDENT, HENCE THIS EDGE IS VERY SHARP.

THE BELT IS NOW ABOUT THE SAME TEMPERATURE AS THE BALL OF FIRE.

illuminated, but not as strongly as in full sunlight. The 'ball of fire' was still too bright for direct observation..."

So how bright was that flash? O.R. Frisch, a member of the coordinating committee, watched from Compania Hill. He filed a report a few days later saying, "Suddenly and without any sound, the hills were bathed in brilliant light, as if somebody had turned the sun on with a switch. It is hard to say whether the light was less or more brilliant than full sunlight, since my eyes were pretty well dark adapted."

Philip Morrison was at base camp and tried to take into account the vagaries of personal observation. He said, "I observed through the welding glass, centered at the direction of the tower, an enormous and brilliant disk of white light." He later qualified that with, "On subsequently looking at the noon sun through these glasses I have been led to estimate this initial stage of the gadget corresponding to a color much whiter or bluer and a brightness several times greater than that of the noon sun."

Robert Serber watched from Compania Hill and said, "I was looking directly at it with no eye protection of any kind. I saw first a yellow glow, which grew instantly into an overwhelming white flash, so intense that I was completely blinded." Within a minute Serber started to regain his vision.

Another perspective was provided by Luis Alvarez who was seated in a B-29 with Deke Parsons flying at 24,000 feet about 25 miles from GZ. He said, "My first impression was one of intense light covering my whole field of vision. This seemed to last for about 1/2 second."

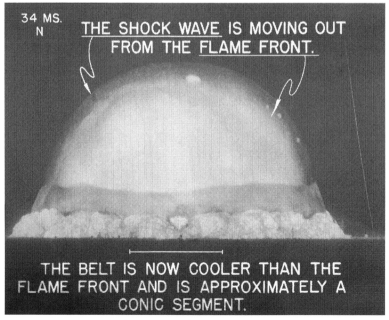

THE BELT IS NOW COOLER THAN THE FLAME FRONT AND IS APPROXIMATELY A CONIC SEGMENT.

Alvarez did not have a direct view of the event because of the clouds that filtered and dispersed the light.

McMillian reported feeling heat during the flash. Marvin Davis, the military policeman, reported it was like opening an oven door to look at what you were baking. Nobel Prize winner Enrico Fermi watched from base camp. He said, "My first impression of the explosion was the very intense flash of light and a sensation of heat on parts of my body that were exposed."

In anticipation of this intense infrared radiation, both Richard Rhodes and Lansing Lamont report in their books that Edward Teller and others at Compania Hill applied sunburn oil to their exposed skin. Yet another hint that these scientists had a very good idea of what was going to happen.

After the initial bright flash, most agree that a huge fireball glowing in shades of red and orange expanded and started to rise. Smoke and dirt were mixed in the flux. It was a boiling, roiling, self-lit phenomenon. Today, a book illustrator might use it to illustrate one of John Milton's levels of Hell in Paradise Lost.

Philip Morrison described it well. He said the white disk stopped growing horizontally and began "to extend in a vertical direction while its appearance had transformed into that of a bright glowing distinctly red column of flame mixed with swirling obscuring matter. The column looked rather like smoke and flame from an oil fire. This turbulent red column rose straight up several thousands of feet in a few seconds growing a mushroom-like head of the same kind. This mushroom was fully

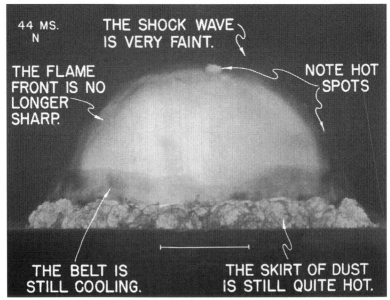

developed and the whole glowing structure complete at about 15,000 feet altitude."

The next step in the process was the radioactive glow. Edwin McMillan reported, "When the red glow faded out a most remarkable effect made its appearance. The whole surface of the ball was covered with a purple luminescence, like that produced by the electrical excitation of air, and caused undoubtedly by the radioactivity of the material in the ball. This was visible for about five seconds."

Cyril Smith, looking from base camp, called the glow a "bluish ionization zone." Victor Weisskopf reported on July 24, "At that moment the cloud had about 1,000 billions of curies of radioactivity whose radiation must have produced the blue glow."

Next came the shock wave from the explosion as it spread in every direction. Most seemed disappointed by its strength. However, Brigadier General Thomas Farrell, Groves' deputy, reported "several of the observers standing back of the shelter (South 10,000) to watch the lighting effects were knocked flat by the blast." They were not injured.

O.R. Frisch witnessed the test with his fingers in his ears. He said, "The report was quite respectable and was followed by a long rumbling, not quite like thunder but more regular, like huge noisy wagons running around the hills." Also at Compania, Edwin McMillan heard it this way: "It was remarkably sharp, being more of a 'crack' than a "boom."

At base camp, Kenneth Greisen said, "I noticed no sharp crack, but a rumbling sound as of thunder." Philip Morrison, also at base camp,

The previous three images were taken at 25, 35 and 44 milliseconds after detonation - very, very early. The photos must have been used by Los Alamos as illustrations in briefings. This image was taken at 8 seconds. All of these photos are from cameras at North 10,000. Los Alamos photos.

reported, "The arrival of the air shock at T +45 on my stop-watch came as an anti-climax. I noticed two deep thuds which sounded rather like a kettle drum rhythm being played some distance away."

Enrico Fermi also watched from base camp but had a different take as he tried to use the shock wave to estimate the yield of the explosion. In his report he said, "I tried to estimate its strength by dropping from about six feet small pieces of paper before, during, and after the passage of the blast wave. Since at the time, there was no wind, I could observe very distinctly and actually measure the displacement of the pieces of paper that were in the process of falling while the blast was passing. The shift was about 2 1/2 meters, which, at the time, I estimated to correspond to the blast that would be produced by ten thousand tons of T.N.T."

By far the most ostentatious observations made about the test were provided by Brigadier General Thomas Farrell and included in the Groves report of July 18.

At one point he wrote, "No matter what might happen now all knew that the impossible scientific job had been done. Atomic fission would no longer be hidden in the cloisters of the theoretical physicists' dreams. It was almost full grown at birth. It was a great new force to be used for

At 15 seconds. Los Alamos photo.

good or for evil. There was feeling in that shelter that those concerned with its nativity should dedicate their lives to the mission that it would always be used for good and never for evil."

Probably because of this kind of verbiage, very few people quote Farrell today. However, I liked his description of the explosion and decided to use part of it on the cover of the missile range's Trinity Site brochure.

As he saw it, "The effects could well be called unprecedented, magnificent, beautiful, stupendous and terrifying. No man-made phenomenon of such tremendous power had ever occurred before. The lighting effects beggared description. The whole country was lighted by a searing light with the intensity many times that of the midday sun. It was golden, purple, violet, gray and blue. It lighted every peak, crevasse and ridge of the nearby mountain range with a clarity and beauty that cannot be described but must be seen to be imagined. It was that beauty the great poets dream about but describe most poorly and inadequately."

There is more. He said the shock wave was an "awesome roar which warned of doomsday and made us feel that we puny things were blasphemous to dare tamper with the forces heretofore reserved to The Almighty."

I can imagine his fellow generals in the Pentagon, dealing with the realities of invading Japan, reading this and shaking their heads wondering, "Who is this guy?" It turns out Farrell had a very interesting background and quite a career.

He grew up on a farm in New York but must have had a knack for science. He attended Rensselaer Polytechnic Institute, a private institution that regards itself as the oldest technology university in the English-speaking world.

Farrell saw combat in World War I and was awarded the Distinguished Service Cross for leading his engineering battalion as infantry in the Argonne battle. The medal is just one short of the Medal of Honor.

His career is filled with interesting positions in interesting locations. We know little of this background because he was at the second level of leadership under Groves and Oppenheimer. Given his assignments before and after World War II, one has to assume he was one of the guys who really made a difference in getting the bombs designed and built.

In contrast to these many analytical accounts is what Felix DePaula remembered. He said that growing up in New York he had never seen any kind of an explosion before. When the bomb detonated in the dark, there were few references and nothing in his memory banks to compare it to. It just didn't move him as it did others.

Observers' accounts of the shock wave vary based on their location. Not everyone heard the "awesome roar." This is understandable since shock waves behave rather erratically. They can roll across relatively flat ground but seem to bounce over some things on the surface. They can be reflected and amplified by the terrain and even by clouds.

For instance, the shock wave did not significantly damage the Schmidt/McDonald ranch house only two miles from GZ. It only smashed windows and doors and broke a few rafters in the roof. The shock wave probably bounced right over the house. If someone had been inside, away from the windows, they might have survived.

Groves, in his July 18 report to the Secretary of War, stated, "The light from the explosion was seen clearly at Albuquerque, Santa Fe, Silver City, El Paso and other points generally to about 180 miles away. The sound was heard to the same distance in a few instances but generally to about 100 miles."

Somehow the terrain and atmosphere seemed to channel the shock wave to the northwest because it rocked Gallup, New Mexico about 170 miles away. During World War II, Fort Wingate, just east of Gallup, was used for munitions storage. The fort has rows and rows of large earthen-covered igloos used for the storage of explosives.

Shortly after 5:30 a.m. on July 16, Gallup residents were awakened by a loud boom coming from the direction of Fort Wingate. Officials called each other and the fire department, gathered together, and headed for the fort. They assumed one of the igloos had exploded.

At the fort they carefully drove every road looking for the damaged

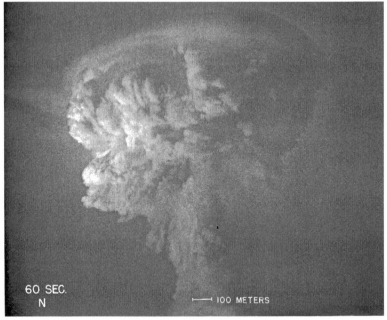

60 SEC.
N
⊢————⊣ 100 METERS

This is a photo of the mushroom cloud at Trinity that doesn't get used much. As indicated, it was taken one minute after detonation. Los Alamos photo.

igloo. The igloos were all intact. The officials were mystified until the news of the Trinity test was released after the first bombing of Japan.

But on July 16 Gallup officials, as well as everyone else in New Mexico, heard a different story from an official news release issued by the Alamogordo Army Air Base. It was one of many prepared by the Manhattan Project to cover a number of possible outcomes.

This release said: "Several inquiries have been received concerning a heavy explosion which occurred on the Alamogordo Air Base reservation this morning.'

"A remotely located ammunition magazine containing a considerable amount of high explosives and pyrotechnics exploded.

"There was no loss of life or injury to anyone, and the property damage outside of the explosive magazine itself was negligible.

"Weather conditions affecting the content of gas shells exploded by the blast may make it desirable for the Army to evacuate temporarily a few civilians from their homes."

A Los Alamos scientist who visited Trinity told me the news release didn't fool some of his colleagues from across the country. Instead, it gave those working on the periphery of the project a clue that something big was afoot. He said he received a cryptic telegram from a friend in the Midwest simply congratulating him and the others on a job well done.

One bomb test witness most people are unfamiliar with was Navy Captain Deke Parsons. Although born near Chicago, Parsons' biographer Al Christman pointed out in a *New Mexico* magazine article in 2001 that Parsons spent some of his boyhood in Fort Sumner, New Mexico. He jumped ahead in high school and entered the Naval Academy at the age of 16.

Parsons was an ordnance expert and spent the early part of World War II as the military lead to develop the proximity fuse. The fuse made it possible for projectiles shot at airplanes to explode just before impact. This allowed for a shotgun effect of shrapnel that had a much better chance of bringing the enemy airplane down than the solid bullets that often passed through the plane without doing much damage.

Because of his New Mexico ties, Parsons convinced the project to have the shells tested by E.J. Workman, head of physics at the University of New Mexico at what

Navy Captain Deke Parsons during his time on Tinian. Los Alamos photo.

would become Sandia National Laboratory in Albuquerque. Parsons then introduced the shells to the Navy in the Pacific.

After such a successful project, Parsons expected some sort of combat command. Instead, he found himself back in New Mexico as the head of Ordnance at Los Alamos. He watched the test with Alvarez from the B-29 flying around Trinity Site. After the test he headed for Tinian.

Parsons was onboard the Enola Gay to complete the final assembly of the Little Boy atomic bomb in the bomb bay while in route to Hiroshima.

After the war he was promoted to rear admiral and became the Navy's spokesman on nuclear issues.

General Groves' Assessment

In his message to the Secretary of War, Groves also tried to summarize for leaders in Washington just how strong the blast was around GZ. Two days after the test, he already had a calculated yield for the bomb and told the secretary, "I estimate the energy generated to be in excess of the equivalent of 15,000 to 20,000 tons of TNT."

Groves went on with concrete examples of damage. He wrote, "A crater from which all vegetation had vanished, with a diameter of 1,200 feet and slight slope toward the center, was formed. In the center was a shallow bowl 130 feet in diameter and six feet in depth. The material within the crater was deeply pulverized dirt. The material within the outer circle is greenish and can be distinctly seen from as much as five miles away. The steel from the tower was evaporated. 1,500 feet away there was a four-inch iron pipe 16 feet high set in concrete and strongly guyed. It disappeared completely."

Groves also described what happened to the tower standing over Jumbo. He said, "This tower is comparable to a steel building bay that would be found in typical 15 or 20 story skyscraper or in warehouse construction. Forty tons of steel were used to fabricate the tower which was 70 feet high, the height of a six story building. The cross bracing was much stronger than that normally used in ordinary steel construction. The absence of the solid walls of a building gave the blast much less effective surface to push against."

After this setup, he said, "The blast tore the tower from its foundation, twisted it, ripped it apart and left it flat on the ground." He added, "I no longer consider the Pentagon a safe shelter from such a bomb." Of course Groves should've known, since he built the Pentagon just before coming on board to head the Manhattan Project.

Within minutes of the explosion, two of the three dangers from a nuclear bomb detonation were past. The first two, radiation burst and shockwave, were easily overcome using simple shelters and keeping a calculated distance away from GZ. The third, radioactive fallout, was an

Jumbo and its tower after the blast. This is the tower Groves refers to in his assessment. Carl Rudder's scrapbook.

entirely different story because its movement and distribution were so unpredictable.

The Fallout And Radiation Levels

The fallout of radioactive particles from the mushroom cloud was much more difficult to control especially as the cloud rose higher than expected. Luis Alvarez, flying nearby in a B-29, reported, "In about eight minutes the top of the cloud was at approximately 40,000 feet . . . and this seemed to be the maximum altitude attained by the cloud."

It was high enough that upper level winds tore the cloud apart and carried it in various directions. The teams of soldiers and technicians went to work monitoring the cloud and measuring fallout as it rained down to the north and northeast.

Later, as all the data was put together, the fallout "corridor" proved to be on a northeasterly line from GZ heading toward Claunch, Vaughn and Santa Rosa – New Mexico villages and towns. The center of that line had the highest radiation readings. As you traveled perpendicular to that line (i.e. to the northwest or southeast) the radiation levels dropped and dropped. Also, generally the farther you went away from GZ, the lower the readings.

In his July 18 report Groves said, "It (the fallout cloud) deposited its dust and radioactive materials over a wide area. It was followed and monitored by medical doctors and scientists with instruments to check its radioactive effects. While here and there the activity on the ground was fairly high, at no place did it reach a concentration that required evacuation of the population. Radioactive material in small quantities was located as much as 120 miles away. The measurements are being continued in order to have adequate data with which to protect the Government's interests in case of future claims. For a few hours I was none too comfortable about the situation."

Groves and the rest of the project felt relief because the vast majority of the fallout missed any large concentrations of population. The most radioactive areas proved to be in the middle of nowhere except for a few instances where ranch houses received large doses.

Groves and others were assured the radiation levels in these areas would drop quickly and there was no reason for concern. But, as can be seen in his report, he was obviously anxious about those levels and wanted to make sure he had real numbers if any lawsuits were filed.

In *Project Trinity 1945-1946*, a report prepared by Carl Maag and Steve Rohrer for the U.S. Defense Nuclear Agency, actual readings have been published. According to the DNA report, on shot day a team monitoring radiation levels in a canyon of the Oscuras east of Bingham found a gamma intensity of about 15 Roentgens per hour. Five hours later the intensity had dropped to 3.8 Roentgens per hour. One month after the test, the area was measured again and showed .032 Roentgens per hour. (The abbreviation for Roentgens per hour is R/h)

The Maag and Rohrer report states, "Significant fallout from the TRINITY cloud did not reach the ground within about 20 kilometers (12.5 miles) northeast of GZ. From this point, the fallout pattern extended out 160 kilometers (100 miles) and was 48 kilometers (30 miles) wide."

These numbers offer a dramatic demonstration of how quickly radiation levels drop after a nuclear blast before they level out for the long haul. The canyon levels dropped 75 percent in just five hours. Of course, some of that fallout is still in the canyon, probably buried under several inches of dirt, and is still slightly radioactive. Like GZ today, there is no hazard left unless you eat the contaminated soil.

Other than a few instances, public exposure to radiation in the hours and few days after the 1945 test has largely been glossed over by officials and historians. That may have changed when Thomas Widner and Susan Flack published a paper in the March 2010 issue of *Health Physics* entitled "Characterization Of The World's First Nuclear Explosion, The Trinity Test, As A Source Of Public Radiation Exposure."

They spent years looking through tens of thousands of records relating to the Manhattan Project and came to some striking conclusions. Basically, in the rush to accomplish the test and then using inadequate equipment and procedures to measure radiation levels, some people were obviously overlooked. It turns out a small number of ranchers probably received excessive doses of radiation even by 1945 standards.

Dose levels for the public were not very well defined in 1945 because before nuclear weapons there was little chance for a John Doe to come into contact with much non-natural radiation.

Widner and Flack found that before the test, when the Army surveyed the area for residents outside the test area, they missed several families in isolated areas. Some of these people were then discovered the day of the explosion when radiation survey teams scoured the area following the path of the radioactive fallout.

One of these sites was the Ratliff ranch in Hoot Owl Canyon, subsequently dubbed "Hot Canyon" by Los Alamos personnel. The ranch was on the Chupadera Mesa about 20 miles northeast of GZ. It was occupied by an elderly couple and their grandson.

Near the house, monitors at 8:30 a.m. on the morning of the test were registering 20 R/hr. By 1:30 p.m. the rate was down to 6 R/hr. Perplexed by the high numbers, Dr. Hempelmann visited the site the day after the test and decided the numbers were then not high enough to warrant evacuation. Later calculations estimated the family members probably received radiation doses that exceeded the standards of the day.

But this is only part of the picture. It is a calculated guess at an exposure to the exterior of the body. The much more complex calculation, because of the many variables, is the consumption of fallout materials. The fallout was everywhere. Residents, like the Ratliffs, talked about seeing a fine white ash covering everything outside. If they worked outdoors and stirred it up, they breathed it in. No one from Los Alamos did nasal swabs to measure how much may have entered their lungs and lodged there.

Another way to consume the fallout was by eating or drinking it. For instance, the Ratliffs collected rainwater off their roof for drinking. The night after the test there were rain showers in the area. That means the fallout resting on the roof was probably washed into their cistern and mixed into their drinking water. It probably quickly settled to the bottom, but who knows how the family withdrew their water – from the top or the bottom.

Finally, no one did real medical and scientific follow-up with these ranchers. For a couple of years after the test, Los Alamos personnel discreetly inquired about the health of these folks without cluing them in on their concerns.

Of course, readings at GZ were much higher than elsewhere because of the activated soil that was emitting radiation in addition to fallout in the crater area. According to Maag and Rohrer, gamma intensity at GZ was estimated to be between 600 and 700 R/h. One week later the readings at GZ were down to 45 R/h and at 30 days they were 15 R/h.

These and many other survey readings were collected from all over the test site by scientists and doctors. It allowed the Medical Group to set up barricades around GZ at safe distances and to limit exposure times for those needing to go inside the perimeter. As levels decreased, the barriers and signs were moved in closer to GZ. Before the test they had set an exposure limit of a total of five Roentgens during a two-month period.

To measure how much radiation each individual received, they were required to wear film badges at chest level outside their clothing. These badges measured gamma exposure and were turned in regularly for analysis.

Records were kept on everyone getting anywhere near GZ from July 16 to the end of 1946. Maag and Rohrer found that approximately 1,000 people, to include family members, visited the site in that time. Most did not go inside the fence that was built around the GZ area. In fact, no one officially entered the fenced area in 1946 and therefore no one received an exposure greater than one Roentgen. Of course, that does not account for trespassers looking for souvenirs or a better look.

The same could not be said of those days and weeks immediately after the test. According to Maag and Rohrer, "On the day of the shot, five parties entered the Ground Zero area. One party consisted of eight members of the earth-sampling group. They obtained samples by driving to within 460 meters (500 yards) of Ground Zero in a tank specially fitted with rockets to which retrievable collectors were fastened in order to gather soil samples from a distance. The group made several sampling excursions on 16 and 17 July. The tank carried two personnel (a driver and a passenger) each trip. No member of this party received a radiation exposure of more than one Roentgen."

Another tank was lined with lead and was equipped with a trapdoor in the bottom. This tank made five trips to within 90 meters (98 yards) of GZ to gather soil samples. The passenger would open the trapdoor and scoop up the soil. On two trips this tank drove across actual GZ.

One driver took the lead-lined tank to the GZ area three times and received one of the highest cumulative doses of radiation at 15 Roentgens.

Whatever happened to those tanks is a bit of a mystery. Various researchers trying to track them down have called White Sands but we have no records on them. The more prevalent theories are that they were so contaminated they were buried near Trinity Site or that they were washed and transported to Los Alamos where they were buried.

The two tanks used at Trinity Site. Carl Rudder's scrapbook.

Also on shot day, a photographer and radiation monitor went in to examine Jumbo and photograph damage. They were about 800 yards from GZ from noon to 1 p.m. Their estimated exposure was between one half and one Roentgen.

Again, Maag and Rohrer looked at the safety and monitoring reports and found that by the end of 1945, over 94 percent of visitors and workers had received radiation exposures of less than two Roentgens. There were 23 individuals who "received cumulative gamma exposures greater than two but less than four Roentgens." A total of 22 individuals received gamma exposures between four and 15 Roentgens.

Scientists quickly gathered what information they could from Trinity Site as the emphasis immediately shifted to the war against Japan. Within a few days or weeks, only military police and few others were left at Trinity. They secured the site and monitored visitors entering and leaving.

News Media At The Site

In September, Groves and Oppenheimer took the news media to Trinity Site. A famous photo taken by the Associated Press shows the two of them and others examining one of the buried footings to the tower. In the photo, the once buried rebar and concrete stands about two feet above the crater floor.

In the photo, all of the visitors are wearing booties over their shoes. This was not to protect them from the gamma radiation at the site as gamma rays are as penetrating as X-rays. No clothing could stop that form of radiation.

The booties prevented the visitors from carrying any radioactive dust away on their footwear. In other words, when they left the site, they completely ended their exposure because they weren't carrying any fallout with them.

Oppenheimer and Groves, center, surrounded by officials and reporters, examine one of the tower footings on the crater floor. WSMR photo.

In this age of instant and universal communication brought on by the Internet, a variety of people have posted articles about Trinity Site. In one the author claims that when Groves took the media to Trinity Site, the reporters were afraid to enter because of the news stories coming from Hiroshima and Nagasaki. Supposedly, to allay their fears, Groves ordered his driver to enter GZ. The website reports the driver ended up spending 30 minutes there and supposedly received an exposure of "100 rads." The author claims the driver died a few years later of some cancer due to his exposure at Trinity Site.

First of all, we see a different unit of measurement used by the web author. He writes about rads instead of Roentgens. This can be rather complicated because Roentgens are the units for measuring exposure, rads refer to the absorbed dose and rems are the "dose equivalent." However, we don't need to delve into their differences for this discussion because, when dealing with gamma radiation, they are considered equal - one Roentgen equals one rad equals one rem. They can be used interchangeably here.

This is further complicated by the fact that the above terms are old traditional American units. Now most scientists and medical personnel use "grays" and "sieverts" which date back to the 1970s. In this system, one sievert equals 100 rem and so on.

We know the web author is fantasizing because the records show that

Military policeman Sgt. Omer Loyd poses by a tower footing at GZ later, after things had quieted down at Trinity Site. Carl Rudder's scrapbook.

by the middle of August the radiation levels at GZ were down to 15 Roentgens or rads per hour. When the press visited almost four weeks later, the level would have been even lower. A good estimate might be five rads if they spent the whole 30 minutes at GZ.

There is no way the driver or anyone else visiting GZ with Groves received an exposure of 100 rads in 30 minutes. The only way would be if some sort of black magic was employed.

A few days after the visit hosted by Groves, there was another press visit but it was very low-key in comparison. On Sept. 15-17, 1945, George Cremeens, a young radio reporter from KRNT in Des Moines, Iowa, visited with soundman Frank Lagouri. They were flown to New Mexico by Captain C.L. Rutherford of the Iowa Civil Air Patrol.

During his visit, Cremeens flew over the crater and recorded his comments. Also, he interviewed Dr. Bainbridge, the test director, and Captain Howard Bush. In addition, he interviewed soldiers still at Trinity Site and some of the eyewitnesses in the surrounding communities.

George Cremeens, left, from KRNT Radio interviews Dr. Bainbridge at GZ on Monday, Sept. 17, 1945. Cremeens collection.

Cremeens then traveled back to Iowa and produced a four-part series of 15-minute reports on the first atomic explosion. They aired on Sept. 24, 26, 27 and 29.

A 15-minute segment was compiled from the material and broadcast nationwide by the ABC Radio Network. For his work Cremeens received a local Peabody Award for "Outstanding Reporting and Interpretation of the News." Later he received an "honorable mention" in the national Peabody Awards competition for 1945.

Cremeens contacted the Public Affairs Office in 1986 to request a visit to Trinity Site. After his visit, he provided Public Affairs with copies of his letters, scripts, photos and a tape of the ABC broadcast.

From that material we made a display, with photos, to explain the tape and played it in the Schmidt/McDonald ranch house during open houses. It was his 15-minute network piece. We had to discontinue playing the tape because visitors wanted to stand around and listen to the whole thing. It created a huge bottleneck at the house and made our shuttle bus system to and from the ranch unworkable.

For a year or so after 1945, Cremeens made a name for himself in the Midwest. After the shows aired, he traveled through Iowa and Nebraska giving talks about the bomb and his experiences - and playing the ABC program.

From the script we learned that during his visit, Cremeens entered the Schmidt/McDonald ranch house and commented that as the shock wave went by blowing out the windows, "the suction created pulled all the ceilings down into the rooms." To read the script and other documents, see Appendix E.

Also, he said Captain Bush experienced the bomb explosion from the South 10,000 shelter where he sat outside with his back to the bomb.

While Cremeens interviewed Bainbridge, the onlookers drank beer at GZ. From left to right are: Capt. C.L. Rutherford, Civil Air Patrol from Iowa; Sgt. Simon Lernor, medic; Capt. Howard Bush, camp commander; and Sgt. Carl Dirksen, military police. From a safety point of view, this was probably not a good idea. Cremeens collection.

Bush told Cremeens that the instant of detonation was so bright he had to physically touch his eyes to make sure they were closed.

Finally, for his show on Socorro, Cremeens said they set up their portable transcribing equipment at the town post office. They asked everyone that came by what they experienced on July 16. Cremeens summarized by saying, "Everyone I talked to was awakened by the sound of the explosion."

This is also where he recorded an interview with Mr. Greene, whose daughter was legally blind. Many writers report that she sensed the light from the blast as she was being driven to Albuquerque.

As an aside, Cremeens, being a radioman, would tell audiences he was impressed that at GZ the communications shack containing $4,500 worth of "intricate radio equipment" was vaporized in the explosion.

Writer George Fitzpatrick visited the site later in 1945. His article about the visit appeared in the January 1946 issue of *New Mexico Magazine*.

Fitzpatrick accompanied a party of National Park Service officials interested in the site as a national monument. Captain Bush was their escort and he took them to GZ, the Schmidt/McDonald ranch, South 10,000, West 10,000 and base camp.

Fitzpatrick reported a chalkboard was still in place at West 10,000 showing the location of recording instruments. At South 10,000 Bush showed the group the wiring in the bunker and the switch that was thrown to trigger the bomb. Also, he pointed out where he sat on the ground outside the bunker during the blast.

At GZ, Fitzpatrick explained how they drove to a fence around the crater with an armed guard at the gate. The guard had them sign in and put their entry time beside each name. When they exited, he recorded the time so their exposure was recorded.

In talking to the men at Trinity, he learned that the mess hall was an equal opportunity facility. Every diner carried his dirty tray to the kitchen after eating and cleaned it himself. This included the VIPs who visited.

In a related incident, when Brigadier General Farrell once visited base camp he immediately got out of his normal uniform and donned a pair of work coveralls. The next morning he appeared in the mess hall queue with everyone else for breakfast. He was accosted by an attendant who said, "Hey, soldier, don't you know the Captain don't allow no breakfast unless you shave!" Supposedly the general skedaddled back to the lavatory to shave.

Fitzpatrick related one incident that spoke volumes about Captain Bush. He wrote, "The day we were there Captain Bush received notification of the award of the Legion of Merit for his part in the atomic bomb project. 'I'm not kidding myself,' he said. 'My men got this for me.'"

The Crater – A Pond Of Green Glass

From the very beginning, starting with the scientists, then the news media and then the general public, visitors were all impressed by the glass covering most of the crater. Cremeens aptly described it as a green, brittle, low-grade glass. It was obvious evidence of the tremendous energy released during the test.

Its thickness varied from a half inch to just small slivers. Its color could be gray to grayish green to a deep emerald green. There were other colors like red Trinitite but it was relatively rare. The pieces were usually very porous with many gas bubbles inside. The bottoms were rough and the tops were usually smooth.

For decades the accepted explanation was that the intense heat of the fireball – after all, it was supposedly many millions of degrees – melted the sand on the floor of the crater to create the coating. More on this later.

Over the years most people have described the crater at Trinity Site as a saucer-like depression as opposed to a gigantic hole in the ground. That is only partially true. Groves reported a partially gouged out area in the center.

In a Los Alamos report dated Oct. 3, 1945, Nobel Prize winner Frederick Reines summarized a study of the crater area in terms of "permanent earth displacement." By the way, the men doing the work at GZ on Aug. 12 and 13 were there about three hours and Reines reported the highest radiation dose received was four Roentgens. This is another point of evidence contradicting the web author concerning the Groves press visit in September.

In his results section, Reines said, "The most marked feature of the crater was its great width, approximately 1,100 feet, and its small depth, about 9-1/2 feet at the center." Most of that depth was confined to a small area, about a 150-foot radius out from the tower base. From the outer edge of the big crater to that inner edge there was simply a slight incline down to the center.

Reines concluded all the sandy soil, out to 1,100 feet, was compressed by the pressure of the explosion above. Then, in the inner area at zero to 150 feet, soil was actually gouged out and hurled into the air.

The tower footings, since they were at the very center, would have been at the bottom of whatever crater existed. Reines noted that the tower stubs were 28'8" apart.

Proof that the inner crater area was greatly compressed came in the form of the bases or piers for the four legs of the tower. The top two feet of these bases were burnt off, and they were also pushed down five to seven feet below where they originally stood.

The report suggested digging up one of these bases to see how much damage there was to the concrete and rebar. Reines said this would be important information in trying to build protective shelters in the future.

The recommendation was taken and from Oct. 8 through Oct. 10, four individuals excavated two of the buried piers – the ones on the northwest and southwest corners. They were on the site for three days and their gamma exposures totaled between 3.4 and 4.7 Roentgens.

Such earth displacement and uptake of soil to create radioactive fallout did not happen in the bombings of Hiroshima and Nagasaki because the bombs were exploded about 1,800 feet above the ground. Most people don't realize the Trinity test created a much larger radioactive fallout cloud than either explosion over Japan.

Although part of the new White Sands Proving Ground, Trinity Site remained under the control of Los Alamos until 1948. Fences and warning signs probably did not keep out curiosity seekers. Many of the artifacts

The southwest pier to the GZ tower after excavation for study as suggested by Reines. Note the crust at the bottom of the hole - this photo was taken after a rain storm or the pier was washed down for examination. Los Alamos photo.

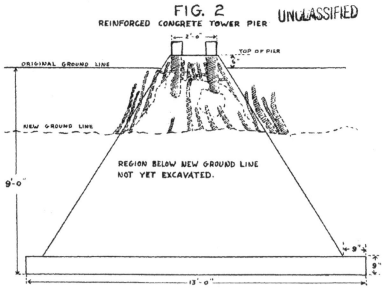

FIG. 2   UNCLASSIFIED
REINFORCED CONCRETE TOWER PIER

ORIGINAL GROUND LINE

TOP OF PIER

2'-0"

NEW GROUND LINE

REGION BELOW NEW GROUND LINE NOT YET EXCAVATED.

9'-0"

9"

9"

13'-0"

Fron Reines' report on the GZ crater.

left on site certainly began disappearing right away.

Public Affairs once received a letter from an individual possessing a

Trinity Site warning sign. He asked if the office would verify its origin so he could sell it as a rare artifact. We declined.

Shortly after the Trinity Site test, the uranium bomb was used over Hiroshima on Aug. 6 and a plutonium bomb just like the Trinity bomb was dropped on Nagasaki on Aug. 9. Japan announced its surrender less than a week later.

After The War Ended

The war was over but a number of soldiers were left at Trinity Site to provide security, maintain facilities, and give support to personnel coming down to conduct studies. According to Felix DePaula, everyone received a bump up of one rank at the end of the war plus a 20-day furlough.

Captain Bush wanted to give the men a longer break after their protracted stint in the desert. There wasn't much for them to do anymore and little hurry to do it. They were bored. They wanted to go home.

So Bush told them as they went on their vacations to send back a request for a 10-day extension, using just about any excuse, and he would grant it. DePaula said he spent a month at home in New York before heading back to New Mexico.

Davis, in one of his letters, said the telegrams with excuses came through the military police orderly room. He said they had a good laugh reading the various reasons offered for a furlough extension.

The author, left, interviews Marvin Davis at GZ in 1990.

There was time for relaxation at the camp as well. In the George Cremeens photos, men are clearly drinking beer. Dave Rudolph, in *Pursuit of Plutonium*, a booklet he wrote about his time at Trinity as an enlisted man, said, "Soon there was an exodus of the visitors, and our base complement faced the task of cleanup and closedown. One of the bonuses from the closedown, was the confiscation by our fire chief of a supply of laboratory alcohol, which he designated a fire hazard and stored at the fire station. He enlisted the assistance of volunteers in our group to help dispose of this fire hazard. This involved our assembling in the fire station with any liquid suitable for diluting the alcohol to a level safe for human consumption."

According to Marvin Davis, Bush invited some women from the Women's Army Corps (WAC) stationed at Los Alamos to help the men celebrate Christmas 1945 at Trinity Site. In a letter to Public Affairs, Davis said about 20-25 women showed up on a bus. He added there was plenty of beer and "most of the women were wilder than the antelope."

Carl Rudder, left, and his buddy Marion (Punch) Harrison pose with the mule deer they shot somewhere around Trinity Site. Rudder's scrapbook.

Also, Bush took company funds and had special rings made for the military police and the engineers who served at the site. Davis said the ring had the words "First Atomic Bomb" on top along with the military insignias for the police and engineers. The numeral one is there under a spur signifying the MP unit was "Detachment One." At the bottom were the words, "silencio servicio" which translates to "silent service."

At a higher level, all military personnel who served in the Manhattan

Project were issued special patches for their uniforms. The 3,500 patches had a blue background that represented the universe. In the middle a white cloud and lightning bolt formed a question mark that symbolized the unknown results and secrecy surrounding the project. The lightning bolt extended down to split a yellow atom that represented atomic fission. A red and blue star in the center of the question mark was the insignia for the Army Service Forces to which the Manhattan Project military were assigned.

Don Montoya worked in the WSMR Public Affairs Office and prepared this rendering of the Manhattan Project patch for our initial handouts.

When Davis left the site in February 1946, there were still a few dozen people there to support any operations that came their way.

In 1946, Los Alamos returned to Trinity with new projects. At the same time, the National Park Service proposed turning Trinity Site into a national monument. The park service recognized the importance of the site, but the idea was rejected by the military. Los Alamos was still using the site, plus it sat in the northern half of the new rocket proving ground. By turning it into a monument open to the public like Yellowstone, the military would have lost the use of the top 20-25 miles of its basic real estate.

Sleeping Beauty

The Los Alamos projects in 1946 revolved around using explosives to crush initiators and measure the output of subatomic fragments like alpha particles and neutrons. To accomplish this they built three underground cells about 1,600 feet from GZ.

In the bunker southeast of GZ, they placed an experiment containing polonium 210 and a light element. The setup used an explosive device to close the electrical switch to turn on equipment and trigger the explosives to crush the two elements.

It was triggered on Sept. 8, 1946. Nothing happened.

Officials decided to leave the experiment instead of running the risk of digging it up. After all, it was buried under 40 feet of sand and the initiator was not a fissionable material. Neither the polonium nor the explosives posed a hazard up on the surface. The test soon acquired the nickname "Sleeping Beauty."

A second experiment in another bunker was successfully conducted. The third bunker was never used.

In March 1967, as the agencies debated the status of Trinity Site, Los Alamos returned to the site to clean up Sleeping Beauty. With the number of visitors growing, someone decided it was time to destroy the high explosives still down in the bunker. Although the explosives were buried deep, it was considered better safe than sorry.

This and other decisions about "safety" at Trinity were usually made for legal reasons. The lawyers didn't want the government held liable in the unlikely case of some sort of accident or claim of injury. They wanted the risk to be as close to zero as possible. Of course, the obvious answer to limiting risk is to close it to the public and bring the risk to just about zero. They lost on that alternative.

Using heavy equipment, crews dug down to the Sleeping Beauty chamber door and carefully pried it open. Inside they found the explosive switch had fired, but it failed to close and start the rest of the experiment.

The team then placed a 100-pound charge in the bunker and destroyed the high explosives and equipment inside. Afterwards they filled the hole and eliminated the mound over both bunkers.

Because of growing public radiation concerns, they also uncovered a small storage bunker about two miles from GZ that contained ten galvanized 30-gallon garbage cans filled with Trinitite. The glass contains a great deal of radioactive material and is the source of most of the radiation at the site. Because of that, it was scraped off the crater floor and buried to reduce the radiation at GZ.

These ten garbage cans were each placed in their own 50-gallon drum and taken to Los Alamos where they are currently buried in one of the lab's disposal areas.

Also in 1946, William Laurence's book *Dawn Over Zero* was published. Laurence was a Pulitzer Prize-winning science writer and New York Times reporter who was the only journalist allowed inside the Manhattan Project. He witnessed the Trinity explosion from Compania Hill.

Laurence may have been given such a unique inside view of the project because of his various articles before the war highlighting the possibilities of atomic energy through fission. One article was classified at the start of the war and libraries were asked to note down anyone asking for a copy of the magazine and report to the FBI. Somebody must have felt he had the vision to document the project's efforts.

On the other hand, theoretical physicist Richard Feynman, in his book *Surely You're Joking Mr. Feynman,* reported Laurence had to ask what the noise was when the shock wave finally hit Compania Hill after the detonation on July 16. Feynman also said he was supposed to show Laurence around the labs but it proved too technical for the reporter.

Later criticism of Laurence was of his almost blind obediance to the whims of the government. When word started to spread about the radiation effects on people in Japan, he toed the line and the downplayed the stories.

Trinity Site Transitions To Local Control

By 1948, research activity at Trinity Site was at a minimum. The Atomic Energy Commission was losing interest in the site, especially since it was smack dab in the middle of the White Sands test ranges. On Aug. 10, 1948, a memorandum of understanding was signed between the Atomic Energy Commission and the Air Force concerning the disposition of Trinity.

The agreement was with the Air Force and not the Army because, at that time, control of the White Sands real estate was still divided between the two services. Holloman was growing into a missile test facility for Air Force programs. They were using the east side of White Sands up through the north end where Trinity Site was located.

Before the Air Force was to take over the area, the AEC was required to erect a chain link fence to encircle GZ at a radius of 1,500 feet. That fence is still there and is what is now called the "outer fence." They were to "erect appropriate signs in and about said Trinity Site, warning trespassers to stay off the property."

Also the commission was to remove "all personal property." We haven't seen any records on when base camp buildings were removed, but this may have been the point in time.

The agreement called for the Air Force to assume responsibility for maintaining fencing and signage, and for protecting personnel from safety hazards.

All of that changed in 1952 when the military "integrated" the proving ground, putting all the real estate and the testing mission under the control of the U.S. Army. At that point all the lands controlled by the Air Force, to include Trinity Site, were transferred to the Army.

Following through on a plan that was devised the year before, in March 1952 the AEC announced it was letting a contract to have the Trinitite at GZ cleaned up. The AEC's announcement created a flurry of public and government interest in Trinity Site. Many people in New Mexico didn't want the site "cleaned up." They felt it had more value as a historical site if the original crater was left alone.

Los Alamos fought cleaning up the crater, saying there was no scientific reason to clean it. The risks were not great enough to warrant the effort.

Visitors and historians have wondered for decades what the crater was like in 1952 when the AEC made their announcement. Based on all the accounts of people sneaking into the site to steal the glass, we thought there might not have been all that much left. Nobody knew for sure. Then, in early 2013, I received a couple of scanned slides from Bob Alley.

Alley was a "broomstick scientist" stationed at White Sands in 1951 and 52. He worked on the V-2 project and as a draftee corporal was in charge of the last flights. He and a couple of friends visited Trinity Site in April 1952. They were able to get to the crater through a hole in the fence and Alley snapped his two photos.

Not only do they show the ground still almost covered with large chunks of glass, they are in color. The substantial area of vibrant green is remarkable. Unfortunately, the original slides are significantly damaged by age, but they energized the small community of Trinity geeks trying to pin down every possible detail of the 1945 test.

This photo of George Cremeens picking up Trinitite at GZ on Sept. 17, 1945 shows the crust of glass. Behind him the ground looks much darker. This is probably some of the asphalt that was put down around the tower to keep the dust down. The same asphalt is visible in aerial photos of the site. Cremeens collection.

In the end, it was an all-too-common legal angle that motivated the AEC to deconstruct the site. In a July 1951 letter to Los Alamos, Dr. John Bugher, the Deputy Director of the Division of Biology and Medicine for the AEC, said they didn't care about the science – it was a "medico-legal" decision. He said their main concern was about being sued. Basically, he said a jury could find in favor of someone claiming their lung disease was caused by Trinity Site no matter how much science was brought to bear. Cautious lawyers and upper-level managers went for the "safe" solution.

On March 10, 1952, U.S. Representative Antonio Fernandez of New Mexico introduced H.R. 6953 to establish a Trinity Atomic National Monument.

On April 3, 1952, a conference was held in Washington, D.C. concerning Trinity Site. It was attended by members of Congress from New Mexico and representatives from the Department of Defense, the AEC, and the National Park Service.

One thing they eventually agreed upon was protection for a portion of the original Trinitite on the crater floor for a future exhibit. The AEC was going to have its way. In cleaning up the site, Trinitite outside the planned protected area was to be removed in "the interest of public health and safety."

Key players then met at a field conference on May 20, 1952 at Trinity Site. Attendees included several reps from the National Park Service, the AEC, and the commanders of Holloman and White Sands.

Out of this meeting came an agreement to protect the sample plot of Trinitite already under shelter about 250 feet west of GZ. The plot was estimated at 20 x 50 feet. At the time the shelter was basically just a roof on poles. The agreement between the parties was to better protect the green glass by adding sides to the shelter down to the ground, thus creating a wooden box over the area.

They also agreed to protect the "wrecked tower" by fencing it to keep out unauthorized persons. This is a reference to the Jumbo tower. Obviously, somebody didn't pay much attention to the agreement as the tower disappeared in the 50s and Jumbo lost its outer bands of steel. Then White Sands tried to give Jumbo away in 1960 – either to be a good neighbor with Socorro or to rid themselves of a perceived nuisance.

The National Park Service efforts in 1952 to protect Trinity were as unsuccessful as those in 1945, 1946 and later years. Each National Park Service probe was countered by the Department of Defense with, "the area around Trinity Site is essential to the defense of the country."

There was no way Trinity was going to become a national monument open to the public every day. Such a move would have crippled the missile range. The biggest asset White Sands has is its large empty space – no tourists in Bermuda shorts driving hither and yon. The emptiness allows violent things to happen in the sky with big chunks of jagged, deadly debris raining down indiscriminately. No one is in danger and no property is damaged.

Protecting the Site

It is probably safe to say many generals commanding White Sands have viewed Trinity Site as nothing but a sore on their backsides. It is not part of their mission, so they get no credit from higher headquarters for doing anything there. Because they receive no funding or manpower to do anything at Trinity Site, they run the risk of criticism or censure if they divert funds or workers for improvements.

It is not surprising that White Sands commanders let the Jumbo tower disappear and almost let Jumbo follow suit. In the 60s several of the Trinity bunkers, including the main control bunker (South 10,000), were bulldozed and burned. The reason given was they were unsafe. In any large organization, be it military or civilian, it is always hard to argue against safety claims – you look like a barbarian if you do.

The South 10,000-yard bunkers (there were actually two structures left) were constructed of wood with sand piled up against their walls. In July 1965, personnel bulldozed the sand away to expose the wood supports and walls. They then sprayed the wood with diesel fuel and lit them up. The WSMR photo archives contain some nice color footage of the event. Those dry timbers survived an atomic bomb but couldn't escape a few gallons of fuel. They burned fiercely on a windy day.

The National Park Service called the destruction an "irreparable catastrophe."

These are the two bunkers at South 10,000 that were destroyed in the 60s. The front one is the control bunker for the whole test. The back bunker was for power - it housed a large generator. Los Alamos photo.

That happened while Major General J. Frederick Thorlin was commander. He happens to be the same general who ordered the lava obelisk constructed to mark the precise spot of GZ at Trinity Site. Some say the general put up the obelisk to improve the site. Others say it was a clever way to immortalize himself.

The obelisk sits between what would have been the four legs of the tower. The lava rock came from the lava flow on the east side of the Oscura Mountains where the missile range's Oscura gate is located. The lava is only a few thousand years old and originates from just north of U.S. Highway 380.

According to Dan Duggan who was an officer on Thorlin's staff, the bronze plaque for the obelisk came back from the foundry with a misspelling in it. It had to be sent back and remade. Since time was of the essence, they had to fly it back and forth.

Duggan said the delay was almost disastrous. Thorlin left WSMR at the end of July 1965 and had scheduled a little ceremony at Trinity to dedicate the obelisk and plaque. Duggan said they had to work the night before to finish the obelisk and get the corrected plaque mounted.

We know the obelisk was complete and had the plaque on it by mid-July because the Wind and Sand newspaper ran a photo of it on July 16, 1965. However, it is a poor picture and half the plaque is cut off. It looks like the date may be wrong, but it is hard to tell from the newspaper. They must have sent it back after that photo was taken.

The plaque says, "TRINITY SITE – WHERE -- THE WORLD'S FIRST – NUCLEAR DEVICE -- WAS EXPLODED ON – JULY 16, 1945."

Given the fact that one of the most important artifacts at Trinity Site, the control bunker, was torched on Thorlin's watch, it seems possible he might not have ordered the obelisk as an altruistic act.

Here's another clue. At the bottom of the plaque, in admittedly smaller letters but taking up almost 25% of the plaque, it is written, "ERECTED 1965 -- WHITE SANDS MISSILE RANGE -- J. FREDERICK THORLIN -- MAJOR GENERAL US ARMY -- COMMANDING." Basically it was his official signature block.

Over the years I took a lot of Trinity Site scientists and support personnel on visits to GZ. A common question was, "Who in the hell is General Thorlin and what did he have to do with the Manhattan Project?"

Also in the July 16, 1965 issue of the *Wind and Sand*, the missile range's weekly newspaper, was a short science fiction allegory concerning Trinity Site. It was written by Hi Anderson with a headline or title of, "Did 1st Nuclear Blast Signal World's End."

The scenario is a space ship exploring earth. They say earth is a "lifeless planet" that no ship has landed on in a thousand years. The crew detects a rectangular metal object below and they descend to check it out.

At the end the commander files this report in his log, "Space time 6-1-1500 Atomic War Year, on the planet called earth, in a northern latitude was located a metal plate bearing the following legend, "Trinity Site where the world's first nuclear device was exploded on July 16, 1945. Erected 1965 White Sands Missile Range . . . and the rest of the writing was destroyed by weathering."

National Park Service Tries Different Tactic

The next White Sands commander fought another perceived Trinity Site battle in the ongoing war with the National Park Service. On December 21, 1965, the Park Service lowered its expectation of getting Trinity as a national monument and placed the site on the National Historic Landmark list. A letter notified the Secretary of the Army that Trinity Site was on the list.

The historic landmark program began in 1960 and recognizes buildings, sites like Trinity, other structures, objects, and districts for their historical importance. For instance, in New Mexico, it includes Kit Carson's house, Taos Pueblo, the Santa Fe Plaza, Ernie Pyle's house and the V-2 launch complex at White Sands Missile Range. Nationally there are about 2,500 properties.

Under the program, recognition is provided by the National Park Service, but it has no control over the properties. In fact about half are private property. For instance, if an owner decides to tear down the historical property, the Park Service can't interfere. The owner simply loses the designation.

It is a little more complicated for landmarks on federal lands because most agencies (the Army in the case of Trinity Site) have regulations in place to support the landmark status by preserving and protecting it.

When the letter from the Park Service about Trinity got to White Sands, Major General John Cone was commander. Paranoia struck the staff at White Sands.

One memo stated making the site a landmark was just the first step in the Park Service's plot to make the site a monument with unlimited public access. Some of these top officials actually thought the Park Service was scheming to close down White Sands Missile Range to get monument recognition – and that the rest of the world would somehow let it happen.

In my 30 years at White Sands, I noticed this was a very common perception. Staff and command were always fearful of encroachment of any kind. Cooperation with non-military agencies and, in some cases, other military organizations was usually seen as surrendering control. These historical programs, endangered species programs, and other endeavors always had WSMR officials wringing their hands saying, "they are going to shut the place down."

In his February 1966 response to the designation, Cone said, "We are protecting the site. Hence we are carrying out the spirit of the Landmarks program as well as the letter and spirit of the Historic Sites Act." This, of course, was just seven months after WSMR burned the control bunkers.

But, mainly, Cone relied on the safety and welfare argument. He appealed to the growing American fear of radiation. A long paragraph in Cone's letter talked about radiation levels at the site and quoted federal regulations about exposure. He said, "Understandably, the need for limiting access to any radiation source is obvious."

Eventually, both sides recognized Trinity Site as a "historic landmark." In 1975, 10 years later, a bronze plaque was added to the obelisk acknowledging that fact.

The plaques on the GZ obelisk during the 1975 open house - the historic landmark was added and the Park Service participated. WSMR photo.

Since then there haven't been any overt efforts to get Trinity Site turned into a national monument. The probable reason is found in a 1973 letter from Major General Arthur Sweeney, Jr., White Sands commander, to the New Mexico Environmental Improvement Agency. In the letter Sweeney said, "United States Senate Bill, S-288, January 12, 1967, authorizes the transfer of Trinity Site to the National Park Service, Department of Interior, upon the termination of the Army military use of the area and when such a transfer is consistent with National security." The Park Service simply was never going to get any commitment firmer than that.

As time passed after the test at Trinity, scientists and medical researchers learned more and more about radiation and exposure effects. The standards imposed in 1945 were replaced with stricter and stricter standards as the decades unfolded. Awareness was also growing and the general population became more fearful as some research showed long-term exposure at low doses could make you sick. General Cone's use of radiation hazards in his letter may have been a result of this.

On March 30, 1966, Cone was returning to White Sands from a speaking engagement in El Paso when he and his driver came across an accident along an empty stretch of War Highway. Cone found a soldier seriously injured and trapped under the wrecked vehicle. The general and his driver tried to lift the car off the victim but Cone, who had a heart condition, suffered a heart attack and died. The accident victim was eventually rescued.

In October 1966, Major General Horace Davisson took command of White Sands. Davisson picked up on Cone's concerns about Trinity Site and he asked the Atomic Energy Commission to look into the safety of the site.

Radiation Risks At Ground Zero

This triggered the 1967 efforts by Los Alamos to clean up Sleeping Beauty, remove the cans filled with Trinitite, and survey the area again for radiation safety. The survey was quite extensive, involving systematic measurements for most of the area inside the Trinity Site fence and outside as well.

In his April 17, 1967 report, Charles Blackwell stated areas outside the fence were the same as background radiation for that area of New Mexico. Inside the fence, levels were highest near the very center of the crater with diminishing levels as you walked outwards.

He said, "Briefly, the levels vary with distances from Ground Zero with a level of 2.5 mR/hr (milliroentgen per hour) out to the fence where the level is reduced to .03 mR/hr. There are a few spots within this area that will read up to 3.5 mR/hr where the concentration of Trinitite is fairly heavy."

He pointed out that all personnel wore film badges to measure their exposure while working around Trinity Site. He said, "The two personnel that were exposed within the area for the greatest length of time were Jack Richard and Gerald Eagan of H-1 as they spent about 85% of the 10 days within the fenced area making the survey."

Earlier, when talking about radiation levels in 1945 and immediately after, the scientists were using Roentgens. A milliroentgen is one one-thousandth of a Roentgen. In other words, an exposure of 3 milliroentgens is .003 Roentgens.

So how much radiation did Richard and Eagan receive? The threshold of the badges they wore was 20 milliroentgens - they had to receive a cumulative dose greater than 20 mR to even be detected by the badges. The threshold was not reached for either man.

To put that in perspective, various organizations now estimate the average American receives about 300 - 400 mR per year in exposure from natural and medical sources.

Blackwell concluded with a reference to one of those natural sources. He said, "I feel that the area was left in a safe condition from an industrial safety viewpoint and considering the amount of radioactivity found within the area that personnel could be exposed to by just visiting the area would be very small. We have checked many pieces of ore brought into this office from weekend hikes in the back country that showed much higher levels of radioactivity than would be found at Trinity Site."

On April 26, health physicist Fred Fey at Los Alamos filed a report using the same data. Given a visitor's proclivity to wander around the site instead of sitting in one spot for eight hours, he concluded "The whole body exposure rate received by a person visiting Trinity Site would probably average no more than 1 mR/h."

Since much of the radiation at Trinity is in the form of alpha particles, it is not particularly dangerous. Alpha particles are stopped by the dead outer layers of skin. A person would have to ingest a large quantity (about 400 grams or almost one pound of Trinitite according to Fey) to have enough remain in the body to become a hazardous source. Experts and most reasonable people I've talked to consider it unlikely that a human would be able to consume a pound of the sandy glass.

Fey concluded, "After a thorough evaluation of the data gathered during a survey of Trinity Site, it does not appear that anyone could receive any radiation injury through a visit to Trinity Site."

In a June 23, 1967 letter, the Atomic Energy Commission reported back to White Sands. Author L.P. Gise talked about the federal regulations and pointed out that the few spots at Trinity Site measuring 3 mR/h exceeded the national standard for the general public. Things were certainly different from 1945 where such a reading would have been background noise.

Gise wrote, "In view of this regulation, and especially the part listing a maximum radiation level of 2 mR/h, I do not believe that the entire area should be opened up for unrestricted access." He added, "I agree with the LASL that visitors to the proposed national monument would not, under any credible circumstances, receive a significant exposure of ionizing radiation."

Gise suggested that another fence be used at Trinity Site to encircle the area with radiation of 2 mR/h or greater. He proposed this as a restricted zone where visitors would only visit for short periods of time.

The missile range responded to this suggestion with an inner chain link fence imposed on the crater area that is 700 feet long and 400 feet across. The shape is more of a racetrack than a circle. Its intent is to better control visitors to the site and limit their time at GZ to about 90 minutes. With all the visitors inside the fence, military police and others could prevent visitors from digging up Trinitite or stealing anything else they might find.

By the end of July, the approval for the fence came from Davisson. His staff suggested using excess chain link fencing from the old Nike Zeus missile program. Zeus was an anti-missile missile and developmental testing was conducted at WSMR.

The fencing could have been brought up from the Zeus facilities on the south end of the range or from a nearby site called ZURF. The ZURF site is just a few miles northwest of Trinity. The acronym stands for "Zeus Up Range Facility." The facility was used to launch Nike Hercules missiles

An aerial view of GZ today, looking west. The racetrack fence is well inside the outer circular fence which is not visible. The black object is the obelisk marking exact ground zero. The other object within the fence is the current shelter protecting an original portion of the Trinitite-covered crater floor. WSMR photo.

as targets back to the south. It would have been a very convenient site to scavenge.

In September 2009, Austin Vick, once chief of data collection in National Range Operations at the missile range, confirmed the fence was simply moved from ZURF to Trinity Site.

Another Question About Safety

After all this, in October and November 1972, Charles Hyder made a rather big splash in New Mexico by publicly criticizing the Atomic Energy Commission for being lax on the dangers of radiation. In particular, he said visitors to Trinity Site were at risk from being there and from the pieces of Trinitite they took away with them. He demanded the state of New Mexico investigate.

Hyder made a name for himself in the decades after this by criticizing government and industry for polluting the planet and endangering all life on the planet. In 1986, he began a long fast in Washington, D.C. to protest war. In 1999, he started what was supposed to be a "terminal fast" in Carlsbad, New Mexico to protest the Waste Isolation Pilot Plant where radioactive waste was stored.

The news media ran with his Trinity Site accusations; suddenly everyone was trying to explain radiation and how it is measured. In June 1973, the New Mexico Environmental Improvement Board responded by voting to investigate "health hazards associated with public visits to Trinity Site."

In his criticism of the government, Hyder seemed most intent on the pieces of Trinitite visitors stole during each visit to Trinity Site. He claimed visitors were not warned about it.

In response, the missile range published the news release and a handout used for the Oct. 1, 1972 Trinity Site open house. Under "Rules and Restrictions," number three stated, "No digging is permitted in the area," number four stated, "Visitors may not pick up objects in the area," and number seven stated, "Visit is restricted to one and one-half hours after time of arrival at Trinity Site."

Finally, in August 1973, a staffer from the Environmental Improvement Agency visited Trinity Site to make his own survey.

Soon afterwards the agency concluded, "Public visitors to the site who obey the rules established for their control will receive insignificant radiation exposures."

The uproar moved officials at the missile range to make more improvements to the site. At the end of November 1972, WSMR erected a barbed wire fence corridor from the outer fence to the gate at the inner fence. This helped to better control the visitors by further confining where they could go. There was to be no more wandering about inside the large outer fence. On the surface, it was a move to protect visitors from themselves, but it also protected the government from accusations of not doing enough to protect folks from themselves.

Of course, the basic problem here is rooted in human nature. Tourists love souvenirs. When not buying them, they are picking them up – rocks, plants, furniture, pieces of buildings, almost anything not nailed down, can disappear with a tourist.

Years ago, when I was the coordinator for Trinity Site open houses, I got tired of so many people stealing the Trinitite. The obvious pieces on the surface were getting harder and harder to find.

I had a sign fabricated that now stands right at the gate to the inner fenced area. Everyone entering has to pass by it. The sign states that removal of Trinitite is theft of government property punishable by fine and/or prison time. Did that, what I consider a fairly clear warning, stop visitors from collecting Trinitite? Nope.

We also stationed Department of Defense police inside the inner fenced area to discourage the theft of Trinitite. Does that work? Nope. Some visitors actually bend down to pick up pieces of the green glass right under the watchful gaze of an officer.

Some people visiting Trinity Site collect the strangest things. I know of two instances where we had visitors stealing the toilet paper out of the porta-toilets on site.

A few people must feel some guilt after taking Trinitite because periodically we'd receive some back in the mail. In one box there was a letter from a young man in Gaithersburg, Maryland. He said, "While within the circular fenced in area where the bomb was detonated, I picked up from the path the enclosed rocks which probably are Trinitite. This was despite the posted warning...."

Interestingly, he wasn't even sure it was Trinitite. This is quite common. There are usually a few visitors who come up to us and ask, "Is this Trinitite?" Sometimes it is, sometimes it is just a chunk of limestone and sometimes it is a pile of rabbit droppings. They usually drop the rabbit poop very quickly when informed what they are holding.

The kind of safety controversy stirred up by Hyder put Trinity Site in the headlines and made more people aware of the site. During the 1970s, the number of visitors rose and soon missile range personnel were dealing with a thousand people at each visit. During the 30th anniversary year, the October event drew an estimated 2,500 visitors.

The Radiation Numbers – How They Compare

Radiation levels in the fenced, GZ area at Trinity Site are very low. The maximum levels are only 10 times greater than the region's natural background radiation. Many places on earth are naturally more radioactive than Trinity Site.

The radiation comes from the nuclei of individual atoms of several different elements. Not only are different elements involved, but there are several kinds of radiation – some harmful and some less so. These different radiations are called "ionizing" and they are harmful when they strike and alter atoms in our DNA and cell structure. The resulting damage can cause physical injury and can lead to cancer development.

Health physicists are concerned with four emissions from the nuclei of these atoms. One of these radiations is the alpha particle that is relatively large and travels fairly slowly compared to other atomic particles. Alpha particles are composed of two protons and two neutrons. They travel about one to three inches in the air and are easily stopped by a sheet of paper.

Another radiation is the beta particle, basically a very light electron that moves at less than the speed of light. These particles are more energetic than alpha particles, but can be stopped by a thin sheet of metal or heavy clothing.

The third form of nuclear radiation is the gamma ray. This is a type of electromagnetic radiation like visible light and radio waves, but is on the energetic end of the spectrum next to X-rays. They travel at the speed of light. It takes at least an inch of lead or eight inches of concrete to stop them.

Finally, neutrons are emitted by some radioactive substances. Neutrons are very penetrating but are not as common in nature. Neutrons have the capability of striking the nucleus of another atom and changing a stable atom into an unstable and, therefore, radioactive one. Neutrons emitted in nuclear reactors are contained in the reactor vessel or shielding and cause the vessel walls themselves to become radioactive.

Americans, even military officials, aren't very good at dealing with these different terms. In 2013, Fort Bliss officials had a possible contamination issue in a bunker once used to store nuclear weapons in the 1950s. One of them tried to reassure the public and said "no gamma particles" were detected. That is the same thing as saying, no "sunlight particles" were detected. What he wanted to say was that no particles of radioactive material that emit gamma radiation were found in the bunker.

Radioactive elements emit various levels of these radiations until they have reached a stable state. For some man-made radioactive materials, this occurs in a few seconds. For other elements a small amount can emit radiation for thousands of years. As they break down they turn into other elements – just like the Germans discovered in splitting uranium and finding barium.

At GZ, the elements emitting gamma rays and alpha and beta particles are europium, cesium, cobalt, strontium and plutonium.

Every American has a different level of exposure each year. On average, the experts now say we average about 300 millirem per year without any medical exposure. When I had appendicitis, I was given a CT scan of my abdomen. The exposure was about 1,000 millirem but the immediate results got me into the hospital within an hour for emergency surgery.

Here are some typical radiation exposures per year for Americans according to the American Nuclear Society, the Environmental Protection Agency and the U.S. Nuclear Regulatory Commission:

*One hour at Trinity Site GZ = one half mrem
*Cosmic rays from space = 50 mrem at Denver, 24 mrem at sea level
*Radioactive minerals in rocks = 63 mrem on Colorado Plateau
*Radioactivity from air at home (radon) = about 200 mrem
*Eating = 30 mrem
*Stuff in your own body = 40 mrem
*A chest X-ray = 10 mrem
*A CT head scan = 200 mrem
*Watching television = less than one mrem
*Smoking half a pack of cigarettes every day for a year = 18 mrem
*Porcelain crowns or false teeth = 0.07 mrem

Even with this kind of factual information, many Trinity Site visitors allow their emotions and fears to trump any kind of logic or reason. In 2009, after an open house, we found three pairs of good athletic shoes, with socks, laying together in the parking lot. We didn't think it likely that all three people would forget their shoes. Instead, we concluded the visitors were afraid to take the shoes and socks home because they might have tiny quantities of radioactive dust on them from walking at GZ.

This is a perfect example of how little Americans know about radiation or science in general today. For years the missile range has tried to educate visitors by having a radiological display at each open house. The display is manned by missile range technicians who use different instruments to measure the radiation emitted by many common, everyday objects.

A typical setup has a pack of cigarettes, a banana, a home smoke detector, an old Fiestaware plate, pieces of colored glass, a telescope lens made with thorium incorporated into the glass and a piece of Trinitite. The technicians lecture on the different types of radiation and how common they are. Also, they run a Geiger counter over the items to show how radioactive each is.

Years ago, technician Robert Huffmeyer had his thyroid gland destroyed with radioactive iodine for medical reasons. The procedure was done before an open house. All day Lisa Blevins, another rad-health technician, ran the instrument over the items on the table. Each object would cause a weak clicking from the device. Then she put the monitor up to Huffmeyer's throat and the clicking went to a loud and constant buzz. Huffmeyer's thyroid was the hottest thing at Trinity Site that day.

Robb Hermes holds up a telescope lens at the Trinity education table. The glass is made with small amounts of thorium, a naturally occurring radioactive element. Thorium allows for a flatter lens that weighs less and takes up less space. Hermes is one of the researchers who came up with the Trinitite-as-rain explanation. Author's photo.

In 2010, I escorted astronaut Leroy Chiao to Trinity Site for a visit. When Chiao was with NASA, he flew three space shuttle missions and then spent six months at the International Space Station in 2004-2005 for his fourth mission into space.

We talked about the fact that astronauts receive much higher doses of radiation than the rest of us on the earth's surface. He said that while in the space station there was a solar flare that set off the alarms in the orbiting laboratory. On the second day, as the flare was dying down, they were still receiving 10 times their normal radiation exposure.

The earth's atmosphere absorbs much of the cosmic radiation coming at us from space. There is a direct correlation between altitude and the amount of radiation we receive. That is why Denver residents receive twice as much cosmic radiation as folks in New York City.

Given this fact, it stands to reason that people in commercial airliners flying at altitudes around 35,000 feet receive significantly more radiation than people on the surface. For the average passenger, these levels are not significant because they are not up there day after day, week after week. However, for crews that fly several times a week for long periods, the accumulated dose can be higher than that received by many nuclear energy workers.

In the various online radiation exposure calculators, there is often a line for air travel. The amount is usually one half millirem per hour. Conveniently, for comparisons, that just happens to be the average exposure for a one-hour visit to Trinity Site.

Most people are surprised to learn some airline employees and organizations have advocated radiation standards for the crews just like those standards for the nuclear industry – after all, their doses are just as high in some cases. However, the government and the airlines have declined, saying the risk is not great enough.

Open Houses

Most documents and old-timers agree the first real public tour of Trinity Site took place in the fall of 1953. Another one was held on the July anniversary date in 1955 and is usually referred to as a religious service with prayers for peace. By 1960, the tours were annual but they were being staged in October because July was just too hot. Attendance was usually in the hundreds.

Early on, these October open houses were scheduled for the first Sunday in the month. By setting the open house on the same Sunday every year, it was the simplest of tasks to look at a calendar and set about planning for the event. All anyone needed was a calendar for the year they were interested in.

Originally, the open house was held on a Sunday because it was basically a religious pilgrimage requested by church organizations. Eventually it shifted to Saturday as the religious aspect dwindled and Trinity Site emerged as a true historical place. Chambers of commerce replaced churches as the cosponsors.

My first Trinity Site open house was in October 1977 on a sweltering day with a high close to 100 degrees. The rigid structure of the event made it a bit uncomfortable for the visitors.

Visitors met in Alamogordo or at the Stallion Gate to be escorted by military police to Trinity Site.

The two caravans of cars were timed to arrive about the same time at the site. Everyone parked in the large parking lot on the south side of the outer fence. People were then herded down to GZ. There wasn't much to see except the lava obelisk.

When the hundreds of people were crowded into the inner fenced area, someone from Public Affairs stood and gave a briefing about the history of the test. After that, a ceremony was held with remarks by the WSMR commander, comments from a representative from the Alamogordo Chamber of Commerce, prayers for peace offered by a local minister, and a talk by a featured speaker who saw the test.

It was a long time for people to stand out in the sun. In 1977 I saw why people fainted every year.

The very next year I was assigned as the Public Affairs coordinator to organize the open house. Although the Alamogordo Chamber of Commerce was billed as a co-sponsor, the event was a missile range affair. To coordinate the event, I dutifully copied the paperwork from the previous open house, assigning 13 different missile range organizations with their tasks. Requirements ran the gamut from the engineers cleaning up the site and roads; logistics providing water buffalos, buses and other support vehicles with drivers; security manning the gates and escorting the caravans; soldiers providing shade netting and chairs; and finally, we needed those vitally important portable toilets. The document was almost five pages long and ended up requiring a few dozen people to work on a Saturday while putting in many hours of overtime.

Over the years we were able to cut back on much of that support as money and personnel grew scarce.

Ranch House Restoration

Then Major General Niles Fulwyler assumed command of White Sands in September 1982. As an Army officer involved with nuclear weapons earlier in his career, he took a great interest in Trinity Site. When he visited the site, he was appalled at the condition of the Schmidt/McDonald ranch house.

Since 1945, the house had simply been abandoned and left to the elements. When I first saw it in 1977, the doors and windows were missing, some adobe walls inside were collapsing because of the leaky roof, the front porch had collapsed, stucco from the outer house walls was laying in piles, the rock wall around the house was knocked down, and all manner of animals lived in and around it.

If we took visitors over to the house for a special visit, we always had to warn them to use caution. In the early 1980s, for a visit by Japanese officers to Trinity, I drove one car. When we got to the house, we warned them about rattlesnakes and walked up to the back door. Right in the middle of the step was a big bull snake all curled up.

Those officers took one look at him and practically ran back to the cars. They didn't care if it was a harmless snake. They did not go back to the house.

Fulwyler took immediate steps for White Sands to stabilize what was left at the ranch house so it wouldn't fall into further ruin. Then he convinced the Department of Energy and Department of Army to share the cost of restoring the ranch house to its July 1945 condition. He was able to get the National Park Service, with their decades of interest in the site, to do the restoration planning and work.

The Department of Energy was

Major General Niles Fulwyler

involved because the United States established the Atomic Energy Commission in 1947 to oversee all things nuclear. That included the development and production of nuclear weapons.

In 1974, the AEC was split up and the resulting agencies given new names. In 1977, the nuclear weapons research and production function ended up in the new cabinet-level Department of Energy. The Manhattan Project legacy passed on to this new organization.

The Schmidt/McDonald ranch house just before restoration. The windows and doors are missing, the front porch and the chimney have collapsed, and much of the stucco is missing from the outer wall. This photo shows the stone addition on the north side of the original adobe structure. WSMR photo.

The cost was something less than $250,000 and the project was completed in 1984. There was a bit of controversy about the venture in the form of criticism from the ranchers who lost their property during World War II to form the old bombing range that morphed into the missile range.

Former rancher Dave McDonald had snuck onto White Sands in 1982 and reaped worldwide publicity for the displaced ranchers. Many felt they were not fairly compensated for the government takeover.

So, when ranchers heard a quarter of a million dollars was being spent on a single ranch house to restore it as a historical exhibit, they cried foul. Many said the money should have been given to them instead.

In addition to restoring the ranch house, some of the money was used to build a new shelter over the preserved portion of the GZ crater floor. We asked for windows or an opening in the roof so visitors could look in at the preserved Trinitite.

Unfortunately, the Trinitite was safely cushioned by several inches of sand and turned out to be completely invisible. In 1991, archaeologist Bob Burton and I removed the sand from a square foot of Trinitite to make sure it was really there. Later we had several feet uncovered so visitors could see it. Within a year, blowing dust had covered the glass deep enough to make it almost impossible to see through any of the openings.

At that point we decided to forgo trying it again. The Trinitite was so fragile, even using fine brushes to remove the dust did some damage. It wasn't worth risking any further harm when there are nice large pieces on display at the radiological exhibit near the inner gate.

The Schmidt/McDonald ranch house was open to the public for the first time during the October 1984 Trinity Site open house. Interest in the house generated a big crowd that day, matching the record anniversary crowd of 2,500 in 1975. In addition, we still had a ceremony at 11 a.m. with guest speaker Bob Krohn who was a physicist working at Los Alamos for the Manhattan Project.

There was no parking at the ranch house, so we supplied a number of buses to provide shuttle service back and forth from the parking area to the house.

We had an instant problem. Everyone wanted to be at GZ at 11 a.m. to hear Mr. Krohn, plus everyone wanted to catch a bus to the ranch house. With all those people coming in escorted caravans with a single scheduled departure time, there simply wasn't enough time for most visitors to do everything. Meanwhile, others saw what they wanted to see and were ready to go home.

The line to ride the buses quickly crossed the parking lot and created traffic congestion. At the ranch house, a very proud Fulwyler wanted to give small groups of people guided tours of the house, so he could relate its history and what had been done to restore it. People were standing in a line several hundred yards long waiting just to get in the house.

It was all taking too long. It was very obvious to us we needed to change our approach to the open houses if we were going to have such large crowds. We couldn't subject visitors to such long lines and long waits.

The solution was to de-emphasize the personal touch. The main roadblock we encountered was our woeful lack of resources – lack of money, space and manpower. The best and cheapest method was to simply spread the crowd out so our limited infrastructure could work.

In 1986 we added a second open house in April, hoping to move some visitors from October to the spring.

Also, we eliminated the whole ceremony – no more speakers or prayers. After that there was no reason for all the visitors to want to be at the site at the same time. They could visit in the morning or early afternoon.

We had already eliminated the old caravans from the Stallion Gate to the site. Visitors were able to check in and drive themselves the 17 miles to Trinity Site. Eventually, we widened that window from 8 a.m. to 2 p.m. If a visitor showed up anytime between those hours, they would be allowed to drive down to the site. The ones showing up at the end of the day usually experienced a limited visit as everyone supporting the event was tired and either gone or packing up to leave.

Since we could no longer provide briefings for each visitor, we had to resort to signs and handouts to tell the history of Trinity Site. At first, we used temporary signs but eventually missile range archaeologist Mike Maloof got us the money to erect permanent signs at the ranch house, Jumbo and GZ.

In addition, we put together a brochure that is given to every vehicle entering the site. We printed them by the tens of thousands.

The new procedures worked. Then, for some reason, crowds began to grow even more. However, we found we were able to keep up with them using our new system. In April 1989, we set a new record with 3,400 visitors. In April 1992, we saw 3,600 visitors. Outside of peaks like these, the crowds have been fairly consistent at 2,000 to 3,000 people per open house since 1990.

Most of the big crowds were in April. Since the weather is usually worse in April, the only explanation we had was the great amount of activity in October throughout New Mexico. For instance, the October open house is always the same weekend as the Albuquerque Balloon Fiesta and other celebrations throughout the area.

The timing of the April open house has created some problems in that it is sometimes on the day before Easter. When that happens, the office receives many calls from people wanting to know if the site is really going to be open. It does.

Other questions are a bit harder to understand. Debbie Bingham, a co-worker in Public Affairs for almost 30 years, once took a call from someone asking about the day. The caller said they understood the open house was always on the first Saturday in April but this year the first of April was going to be on a Sunday. "Could it be," the caller asked, "that White Sands considers the Saturday before April 1 as the first Saturday of April?" Debbie about fell out of her chair but calmly explained, "No, that would be the last Saturday in March. The first Saturday in April will be on the seventh."

The 50th Anniversary

In 1995, for the 50th anniversary of Trinity, we thought we ought to open the site on the actual day. After all, the 50th anniversary of anything in America is a big deal. However, we greatly underestimated the public's interest in the site. Actually, we totally underestimated their interest.

First of all, we had to get command approval to open the site on the actual anniversary date which happened to be on a Sunday. Then CNN and some members of the public called about being on the site at exactly 5:30 a.m., when the bomb exploded. The news network planned to broadcast live via satellite at 5:30.

We basically set up this open house like the regular ones but eliminated the Alamogordo caravan to cut down on support. By using only the Stallion gate, the plan was to open the gate from 5 a.m. to 11 a.m. With the early morning hours, we thought we could accommodate the few who

The author, left, interviews B-29 pilot Fred Bock in 1995 at GZ during a special tour of Trinity Site for the 509th Composite Group - the folks who dropped the atomic bombs on Hiroshima and Nagasaki. When most people hear that the Nagasaki bomb was dropped from the plane called Bockscar, they assume the person is saying "boxcar." In reality it was the name of this pilot's plane. However, Bock was not flying it on Aug. 9. For the Nagasaki mission Major Charles Sweeney flew Bockscar and Bock piloted Sweeney's plane, The Great Artiste, which was an observation platform for the mission. WSMR photo.

wanted to be there at 5:30 and also get most people off the site before the heat of the day. It might have worked if it had been a Wednesday.

When the day arrived, we expected a hundred people might be waiting at the Stallion gate at 5 a.m. We were very wrong. The line of cars was backed up for miles. We took one look and thought "these people are nuts."

Eventually we counted over 5,300 visitors.

It was also our only real encounter with a group of protestors. Very early on, someone rushed toward the obelisk and threw a red liquid on the monument, saying it was symbolic blood. The military police quickly grabbed the person and carted him off to the Stallion gate.

Still very early in the morning, there was a group of 50 to 60 people who looked, smelled and talked very much the way I remember college students in the late 60s. Eventually, they linked hands to form a circle around the obelisk and chanted as they danced around it. They called for others to join in but everyone just watched. The hippie era is long gone.

The military police wanted to wade in and arrest them all. We asked for restraint since they weren't a threat to anyone and confronting them might have turned ugly. It was not very long before they tired of the song and dance and quietly went away.

By 7 a.m. we were running a quiet and typical open house. Visitors, for the most part, were appreciative of the opportunity to be there on the 16th.

Once in a while, a problem would arise at an open house that no one had foreseen. During the October 1991 open house, only the first 37 cars in the Alamogordo caravan made the turn in the town of Tularosa to go

---

This information is posted at Trinity Site as a sign to give drivers some idea of how far they are from various places in Southern N.M.

MILEAGE CHART

San Antonio to Stallion Gate exit on U.S. 380 ----- 12
Carrizozo to Stallion exit on U.S.380 ----- 53
Highway 380 to Stallion ----- 5
Stallion Gate to Trinity Site ----- 17
San Antonio to Socorro ----- 10
San Antonio to Albuquerque ----- 81
San Antonio to Las Cruces ----- 130
San Antonio to El Paso via I-25 ----- 175
Carrizozo to Tularosa ----- 46
Carrizozo to Alamogordo ----- 56
Carrizozo to El Paso via Highway 54 ----- 146
Trinity Site to Alamogordo w/ the caravan ----- 85

to the missile range gate. The other 120 cars just kept going straight north headed to Carrizozo on U.S. Highway 54.

Apparently, in making its way from Alamogordo to Tularosa through the many stoplights along the way, the 38th car totally lost contact with the car in front of it. Its driver just keep going straight through Tularosa. Many locals told us later they knew it was wrong to head to Carrizozo, but there wasn't much they could do.

Most of the lost visitors made it to Trinity Site anyway by going west from Carrizozo to the Stallion Gate. It was a long drive for them.

We learned our lesson there and asked the Alamogordo Chamber of Commerce to make sure they have someone at the turnoff making sure the whole caravan got to Trinity. A few years later that arrangement led to a different kind of problem with a young woman trapped by circumstance.

Again, the caravan was stopped and pulled apart by stoplights on the way to Tularosa. This time there was an officer at the turn off with his vehicle's lights flashing. He stood by the side of the road and mindlessly signaled cars to turn to the west.

When the caravan arrived at Trinity Site, a young girl, not more than 16, got out of her car shaking and crying. She asked where she was and how was she ever going to get to the wedding rehearsal in Tularosa in time. Plus, she was just about out of gas.

It turned out she got mixed in with all the cars heading north out of Alamogordo, saw the officer, with lights flashing, signaling to the left. She thought something was wrong so she followed the crowd.

Once we assured her it would be all right, we gave her some gasoline and one of the police officers escorted her back to Tularosa. I doubt she made the rehearsal, but she was back in plenty of time to attend the wedding.

Probably the best thing we ever did for the Trinity Site open houses was convince my boss and the Alamogordo Chamber of Commerce to change the caravan starting point to jettison the drive through the minefield of stoplights. It was politically impossible to kill the caravan so we found a way to make it run smoother for everyone.

The suggestion was to organize and start the caravan at the football stadium parking lot on the west side of the village of Tularosa. From that lot it is almost a straight shot on a back road, without traffic lights or traffic, to the missile range's gate.

Because of this change, state police and sheriff's deputies are no longer required – no more lost caravans or hijacked drivers caught up in the rush.

Buddhist Monks Visit

For most visitors Trinity Site is a historical curiosity. They come to see what all the discussion is about.

For some however, Trinity Site is a powerful emotional symbol for them personally. They feel or believe they can pray there, chant there, or engage in some ceremony that will make a difference. We have had people sit or kneel on the ground at GZ and say they are praying to heal the earth. At the very least it makes them feel good.

Those two bombs dropped on Japan killed a lot of people very, very quickly. For decades, people all around the world have feared such weapons might destroy mankind. In America, Christians have been the main proponents for praying for peace at Trinity Site. The U.S. military, like Congress and other government entities, has no problem with "Christian" prayer, so the original open houses started with prayers for peace.

When a similar request came in 2005 from individuals representing a group of Japanese Zen Buddhist monks, officials took a long hard look at the request. Some of us wondered if Buddhist prayer would be allowed. In the end, it was decided these monks were the real deal, and White Sands had no overwhelming reason to deny their request.

Their story was that when Hiroshima was bombed in 1945, the monks lit a fire from the smoldering ruins and kept it burning for 60 years. During much of that time, they trekked all over the world carrying a portion of the flame to promote peace and the end of nuclear weapons.

In Buddhism, 60 years is a complete cycle, like the life of a man. Since the atomic bomb cycle was coming to an end in July 2005, they believed that by extinguishing their flame where it began (Trinity Site) they might end the "nuclear cycle."

So a small group of supporters and the monks were allowed to walk into Trinity Site on Aug. 9, 2005. It was 60 years to the day from when a nuclear weapon was last used on human beings. In a short ceremony at the obelisk, they extinguished the flame to close the circle.

The ceremony was filmed by the monk's support group. A summary video is probably still available on YouTube.

The Real Trinitite Story

Just when you think you know some fact or truth – not believe it, but know it – often something comes along to rock your boat. That is the great thing about science. It allows for better explanations that only require better proof. No holy books need to be rewritten.

That happened to us in 2003 when we got involved with Robb Hermes and Bill Strickfaden from Los Alamos. Hermes was a polymer chemist with the lab at that time and Strickfaden was a retired physicist and independent investigator. Their work has rewritten the story of how Trinitite was formed.

They contacted us and asked for samples of sand from both GZ and an area outside the outer fence. They said they could use the comparative samples to recalculate the yield of the bomb.

And, by the way, they added, could they get some samples of anthill sand from GZ? We said sure, and on the next trip to Trinity Site we filled some quart plastic bags with the appropriate sand and mailed them to Hermes.

Not long after, Hermes contacted us excited about the ant sand. He said there were small balls or spheres of glass mixed in with the sand. In other words, there were tiny beads of Trinitite mixed in. Some weren't much bigger than a pinhead, but some were larger and clearly balls, not shards. People have found larger spheres that are about the size of pearls which are appropriately called "Trinitite pearls."

To see color images of Trinitite beads, look at the back cover of this book.

Hermes said that many of the sample chunks of Trinitite stored at Los Alamos were shiny and smooth on top but rough and irregular on the bottom. On some of the pieces, spheres were clearly embedded in the mixture. In fact, in some cases the rough bottoms were simply spheres stuck together.

The theory accepted for 60 years on the formation of Trinitite was that the fireball simply melted the surface of the crater and turned it to glass. Kevin Casey, who was in Public Affairs at the time, called it the "Trinitite crème brulee effect."

This explanation did nothing to account for the spheres.

Strickfaden said he modeled the explosion knowing the height of the tower at detonation, the bomb's basic yield, and the kind of sand found at GZ. Using different models, he could not get any of them to generate enough heat on the surface to form Trinitite over a half-inch thick. The fireball just wasn't there long enough.

That set them on a course looking for another mechanism to form the glass. When they looked at old reports and photos of the crater, as in the Groves account, they realized quite a bit of material was actually gouged out of the ground. The crater wasn't simply smashed down and compressed forming a nice dinner plate surface.

The two quickly realized that if this material was thrown up into the fireball, the tremendous heat would have melted the sand and turned it to a mist of liquid rock. Maybe it was hot enough to turn some of it into a gas which, when cooled, would reform as a liquid.

At this point, it became something like raindrop physics. Droplets of liquid rock bumped into each other to form larger ones. Eventually, they fell back to the ground. In some cases, the tiny spheres were suspended long enough to solidify and remain beads after they hit. Other drops hit as a liquid and spread, forming puddles across the surface.

"Much of the layer was formed not on the ground but by a rain of material injected into the fireball that melted, fell back, and collected on the hot sand to form the observed puddles of Trinitite, especially within the radius of the hottest part of the event," they concluded in an article for the Fall 2005 issue of *Nuclear Weapons Journal*.

"After falling to the ground, the top surface of the Trinitite layer was still heated somewhat by the fireball and thus developed a smooth surface . . . We calculated an average fireball temperature of 8,430 Kelvin," they reported. That's 14,710 degrees Fahrenheit.

Their theory nicely explains the spheres. It also explains why there was Trinitite found on top of the asphalted areas and on top of fence posts and rocks afterward.

It also explains a note in Reines' 1945 report that asphalt roads within 150 feet of the tower were not destroyed in the blast. In fact, in the aerial photo taken 28 hours after the test and many other shots, the black asphalt is still very evident.

In this process of examining Trinitite, they were able to confirm that the green color of the glass is simply caused by the amount of iron found in the sand. Since ancient times, craftsmen knew how to add iron oxide to liquid glass to tint it green.

In one trip to Trinity with them, we discovered a few chunks of the very rare red Trinitite. Los Alamos analyzed one piece and Hermes reported the red is from copper mixed in with the glass. There were large copper coaxial cables running up the north side of the tower; that wiring is probably the source of the copper. Supporting that idea is the fact that the red glass was found north of GZ.

During the October 2011 Trinity open house, I was answering questions at GZ when a young boy and his father approached me. The man told his son to show me what he had found pawing around in the dirt. The boy held out a glob of Trinitite, not quite a sphere, that was mostly white with just a tinge of turquoise.

In visiting Trinity Site for more than 30 years, I had never seen such a color. I thanked the boy and tucked the Trinitite away for safekeeping. I then sent it to Hermes at Los Alamos for analysis. He reported their quick-look showed the white was caused by calcium, probably from the calcite or caliche in the soil.

Since the initial work on the green glass, Hermes has pursued his quest to learn as much about Trinitite as possible. He has even acquired a piece of glass from the first Soviet test site where Joe-1 was exploded. That glass is a deeper greenish black but has the same texture and qualities of Trinitite including the spherical inclusions on the bottom. Since Joe-1 was a carbon copy of the Trinity event, including a 100-foot tower, it means their glass was probably formed the same way.

Then in early 2010, Hermes discovered a buried Los Alamos report from 1947 that postulated the same theory he and Strickfaden had come up with for the dispersion of Trinitite. This document was classified as "secret" when written, so very few people were privy to the information. If the document had been available earlier, maybe the crème brulee theory never would have grown into the myth it has become.

In addition to their reformulation of the Trinitite story, Hermes and Strickfaden waded into the issue of the size of the GZ crater. Previously I have quoted diameter measurements presented by Groves (130 feet) and Reines (300 feet). Groves has to be forgiven for his lowball estimate as it was made from a distance right after the explosion. However, it should be noted that Bainbridge, in his Los Alamos report *Trinity* said the crater was 30 feet across.

Hermes and Strickfaden examined aerial photos taken of the crater the day after the test. The high-resolution negatives were perfect for enlarging – so much that they could clearly see the four tower footings protruding from the surface.

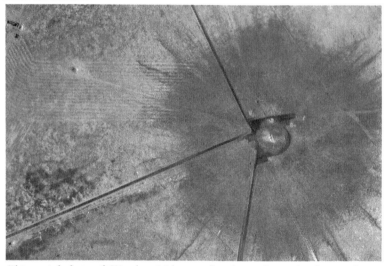

This aerial photo of GZ taken 28 hours after the explosion has been published repeatedly - so much so the quality of the reproductions is fairly low. When you get a copy from the original negative or from one of the Los Alamos scans, there is remarkable detail in the photo. This is what Hermes and Strickfaden used in their crater analysis. The three asphalted roads leading to GZ are clearly there. Where they meet are several triangles - more sheets of asphalt around the tower. There is a circle between the triangles that is where the tower stood. Zooming in on a good image, it is possible to see the tower footings. Up in the top left corner is a tiny white object with a black line leading off the image. This is Jumbo still standing and casting a shadow over the ruin of its tower. Los Alamos photo.

From this and other information in the Los Alamos archives, they calculated the crater had a diameter of about 250 feet (close to Reines' number) and the spread of Trinitite covered a circle with a diameter of close to 2,000 feet. They concluded many people, over the years, have confused the crater with the covering of Trinitite at the site which why you sometimes see the crater estimated at a quarter of a mile.

After all that work, Hermes and Strickfaden never did provide a firm yield for the Trinity plutonium bomb, as their calculations were derived from their observations of the available Trinitite. The result was a rather broad range of yields, including the generally accepted yield of 20 kilotons.

Myths And Misinformation

Over the years we in Public Affairs worked hard to present factual information about Trinity Site and its history. If we made mistakes, we corrected them. However, correcting other people's mistakes proved pretty much impossible.

The news media are always making mistakes. Because the Trinity Site story is a little history and a lot of science, many reporters are not equipped to retell the tale. Some are smart enough to realize it and focus only on the history of what happened.

In 1989, New Mexico Magazine ran an article on Trinity Site, stating the bomb tested was uranium based and not plutonium. This seems like a pretty big oops when you are talking about the very first bomb.

The author also called Jumbo a "bomb casing." Actually this is a very common error. We often hear visitors at the site talking to family or friends explaining that Jumbo is the Fatman bomb casing.

This error seems a bit remarkable when these same people seem astounded that the Schmidt/McDonald ranch house survived the explosion. To them an atomic explosion is so big it destroys everything for miles and miles. Given that belief, I've always wanted to ask how would a bomb casing survive the test?

Years ago, a historian who visited Trinity Site several times wrote a short piece about Jumbo for one of the Smithsonian magazines. In it he told readers that if they wanted to see Jumbo, they would have to go to Alamogordo and enter with the caravan.

He didn't mention the Stallion gate or that 75% of the visitors enter there. I wrote the magazine that the author's directions were a bit like suggesting the best way to see the Washington Monument was to fly into Baltimore first. The distances are similar.

Sometimes writers mess up and make it tough for the public. They have gotten the dates wrong and people show up at the gate expecting an open house. This causes the missile range some bother, but it is pretty minor compared to the folks who may have driven in from Santa Fe or

Denver or Phoenix only to find they can't get in. To say the least, some are quite irate to be turned away.

When the Internet started to grow and Public Affairs established a webpage. We were able to develop a page devoted to Trinity Site misinformation and myths. The idea was to correct common errors and some of the totally bogus information out there.

For instance, there were a number of people regularly selling pieces of Trinitite on eBay. Most of them said the glass was from Trinity Site located in the Tularosa Basin, Otero County or near Alamogordo. None of that is true. So I posted quotes from their ads and web pages along with the correct info. After a while, they started to change their statements and eventually most were at least getting the location correct.

Other myths and misinformation include: the idea that radiation at the site will fog the film in an old-fashioned film camera; that there were soldiers taken to the site on a train and forced to observe the blast from close-in trenches; that you have to pay to get into the site or reserve a spot with some outside organization or company to get in; that the gypsum sands at White Sands National Monument are white as a result of the bomb test; that roadblocks along U.S. Highway 70 during the 1950s were for atomic bomb tests on the missile range; and that you can see GZ while flying on a commercial flight between El Paso and Albuquerque.

Concerning the last myth, I was on a commercial flight where the crew pointed out what they thought was GZ to the east of the airplane – the

A person selling an old postcard of the dunes at White Sands National Monument on eBay stated the sands were bleached white by the atomic bomb test at Trinity Site. Author's photo.

missile range's airspace is off limits to commercial aircraft. What they pointed out was a warhead impact target area on the west edge of White Sands, called Stallion WIT. The target area is graded regularly so it is barren sand. It shows up very well against the surrounding grasslands. GZ is visible but it is covered with grass and much harder to detect, especially from the distance of a commercial airliner.

How Trinity Generated The Roswell Incident

Finally, my favorite myth or story about Trinity Site involves a package I received years ago from Mark Harp in Memphis, Tennessee. Basically he sent a thesis and supporting letters explaining how the earth was really hollow. At one time he even had a webpage devoted to this pet project.

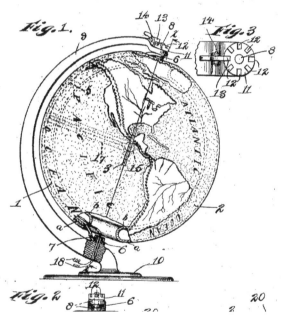

M. B. GARDNER.
GEOGRAPHICAL APPARATUS.
APPLICATION FILED NOV. 25, 1912.

1,096,102.

Patented May 12, 1914.

This is the front page of a patent awarded to Marshall Gardner in 1914. Mr. Harp claims that the hollow earth theory was officially recognized by the U.S. government when it granted this patent - which is readily available on the U.S. Patent and Trademark Office website. However, when you actually read the patent, you learn it is for a mechanical globe to be used by Gardner in promoting his version of the hollow earth idea. They did not award him a patent for the hollow earth theory - it was for a funky new globe.

He said the governments of the world know the earth is hollow and they are keeping it a secret from the rest of us. There is supposedly access to this inner world through large holes at the earth's poles. I'm not sure what keeps the water out of the hole at the North Pole since that pole is in the ocean.

Inside the earth is a sun-like energy source floating in the center of the void and a humanoid civilization living in this subterranean realm. I suspect Mr. Harp saw "Superman and the Mole Men" on television when he was a boy.

His story continues that on July 16, 1945, the atomic bomb explosion at Trinity Site so shook the planet that these humanoids were, hmmm, shaken by the experience. They wondered what it was. Maybe there was some danger approaching.

So they built a flying machine and sent a team out the hole at the North Pole to fly down to New Mexico and investigate. Unfortunately, their vehicle malfunctioned and crashed in the desert northeast of Trinity Site. You guessed it – near Roswell.

Actually, most UFO proponents say the crash site is closer to Corona, New Mexico which is northwest of Roswell. That is where Brazil originally found the foil and rubber debris.

What the rancher and military personnel found when they investigated was not an alien ship from "outer space" but an alien ship from "inner space."

Trinity Adds To Controversial New Theory

Supporters of big budget military research projects often say you never know what non-military information or advancement you might get from the research and development of weapons. For instance, the German V-2 rocket quickened the civilian effort to put a man on the moon, and the Department of Defense's Global Positioning System (GPS) has made an easy and revolutionary move into the civilian world.

In 2012, information gleaned from the Trinity Site test was being used to defend a controversial theory about an asteroid impact that may have almost overnight cooled and dried the planet. The cooling lasted for over a thousand years before the heat was turned up once again.

The asteroid impact theory is a bit controversial and has a lot of opposition. However there are supporters, just like in the early days of the plate tectonics theory, who are rushing to find supporting evidence. At this point, no one can tell if this new idea will have a positive result like plate tectonics.

The story goes something like this. Toward the end of the last ice age 20,000 years ago, the earth began a steady warming program that was running smoothly. Ice sheets were retreating and the average temperature was on the rise. From a modern human's point of view, things were definitely looking good.

Then, 12,900 years ago, there was a sudden hiccup in the big thaw. It is called the Younger Dryas period. Temperatures dropped and much of the planet was plunged into a drought. In England, researchers say the temperature dropped an average of 23 degrees F.

Of course, this wasn't the effect everywhere. Weather patterns were altered and local results were as varied as the different continents. For instance, in some areas there was increased snowfall in mountain ranges, forests disappeared in places like Scandinavia to be replaced with tundra, and in North America human beings may have had some difficulty finding enough to eat as many animals went extinct. Some say the people responsible for the Clovis culture may have declined because of this cooling.

Explanations for what caused the warm-up to suddenly reverse are varied. In 2014, a look at Wikipedia revealed the prevailing theory was linked to a flood of fresh water into the Atlantic Ocean from melting glaciers that, in turn, blocked the northward flow of warm tropical waters. Another explanation was increased volcanic activity may have created a "nuclear" winter scenario. Other scientists propose a solar flare may have altered the atmosphere.

The Wikipedia authors also mention an asteroid impact theory but generally spurn it as highly unlikely with little physical evidence. They also say that much of the impact evidence is filled with errors.

So what is the impact theory and how does it relate to Trinity Site? Basically, it is the nuclear winter idea with an asteroid or comet instead of a hydrogen bomb exchange being responsible for the tremendous gush of dust and smoke into the atmosphere. One problem with this idea is that the event was not long ago. Thirteen thousands years is just a blink in geologic time. If there was a meteor impact, there should be a big crater.

However, two impact events – one here on earth and one in the far reaches of the solar system – triggered the imaginations of a few scientists to see beyond the need for an impact crater. The first event was the asteroid/comet explosion over Tunguska, Russia on June 30, 1908.

When scientists got to Tunguska, they found 80 million trees covering 830 square miles flattened. They also found no gigantic crater.

It took several years, but scientists eventually figured out that something, an asteroid or comet, exploded about three to six miles up with the force of one thousand Hiroshima atomic bombs. And only fragments reached the ground so there was no crater like the huge Meteor Crater in Arizona.

Since then we have learned that both comets and heavy items, like asteroids, can explode in the atmosphere and create the equivalent of a high altitude nuclear burst. With all of the security cameras and dash cams now out there, we regularly see meteorites and sometimes explosions in the atmosphere.

One of the more recent explosions was the meteor impact over Chelyabinsk, Russia in 2013. This rather large meteor had an estimated diameter of about 65 feet. It hit at a calculated speed of 41,000 miles per hour and luckily for everyone below, exploded at the high altitude of 18 miles. The energy released was somewhere in the neighborhood of 500 kilotons of TNT and was mostly absorbed by the atmosphere. It was something like 25 Fatman bombs exploding.

The second impact event that opened eyes was the breakup and collision of Comet Shoemaker-Levy 9 with Jupiter in July 1994. This event provided scientists around the world with a new set of possibilities for planetary impacts.

It was electrifying because it was man's first eyewitness experience of seeing a big object strike a planet. Of even more interest was the fact the comet broke up into many large pieces on approach over a period of about a week.

Because of the timing and the rotation of Jupiter, each comet chunk hit a different spot on the planet. Suddenly, applying the scenario to earth, questions started to bubble up. What if a large asteroid broke up into many pieces and collided with the earth 12,900 years ago in a series of impacts spread around the world creating a series of huge upper atmospheric explosions? If the chunks hit at the right angle, the impacts might leave few craters, if any.

So, the proposal is that the pieces of asteroid were big enough to blast large sections of the planet's atmosphere and leave lots of smoke and dust hanging in the air to create an "asteroid winter." Now the question is, how do you prove these explosions took place?

Robb Hermes, our Los Alamos Trinitite guru, has been pulled into the effort to prove the impact theory because of his research and knowledge concerning the glass formed in the Trinity test in 1945. It turns out that nuclear explosions are similar to high-speed asteroid explosions in that they are hot enough to liquefy minerals and turn them into glassy substances.

This is important because impact proponents report they have recovered glassy spheroids and other blobs from sites in the Middle East, Europe, South and North America. Mostly these glassy items are made from earthen minerals melted during an air burst impact; that is, much like the Trinity event, they explode close enough to the ground and with enough energy to melt the dirt and dust that was raised into the presumed fireball. In some cases, a cosmic chemical signature is also present.

One of the very best places for finding such glassy spheroids, as it turns out, is at the Clovis site in New Mexico, dated to 12,900 years ago. Some naysayers claim the finds are either miss-dated, or were fallout from other natural phenomenon.

According to Hermes, there were obviously no Fat Man atomic bombs 12,900 years ago to make these glass spheroids being found in these locations. Also any other human activities like firing pottery and making glass couldn't generate the heat needed until well into the industrial age.

Scientists have looked at natural possibilities like wildfires, volcanoes, lightning and collisions from space. It turns out, wildfires are not hot enough and volcanoes can indeed produce something similar – think Pele's tears. Lightning is hot enough but its ground impacts are pretty much confined to making fulgurites in very small areas – like a few feet. A lightning strike can also produce an "exogenic fulgurite," which is spatter from a very high energy strike. The spatter droplets look very similar to Trinitite and the Younger Dryas spheriods but differ in chemical composition.

Materials found in association with the Younger Dryas research are spread over miles. In comparing the lightning-generated glass to the samples found in association with Younger Dryas sites and Trinity Site, they are nothing alike.

That leaves the asteroid collision/explosion explanation. It turns out the glasses created in the Trinity Site test match very well with the material found so far on several continents dating back 12,900 years.

As with any new theory or explanation, it takes a lot of evidence and reasoning before most scientists accept it. Sometimes it can go one way or the other very quickly, if the science is good. It will be interesting to see in the next few years if there is enough evidence to feed and nurture this new theory.... or will it simply die because of a better explanation?

Right Or Wrong? Or Is It More Complicated?

Frequently visitors to Trinity Site want to discuss or argue about the use of the atomic bomb on Japan. Sometimes they try to engage the government officials in debate and sometimes they connect with each other. Most are very civil but sometimes tempers flare. During the 50th anniversary open house, the military police had to step in and physically separate three individuals who seemed ready to let fists fly. For some visitors, emotions bubble to the surface at Trinity Site.

Here are some of the arguments I've heard over the years for and against using the atomic bomb over Japan. There are a lot of them. With this many points and counterpoints, the question is obviously not a black and white issue. They are presented in no particular order:

*It was inhumane to target civilian populations.
*The U.S. should have done a demo first for the Japanese government.
*They were ready to surrender anyway and it was not needed.

*The bombings were racially motivated and not a military necessity.

*Fighting month after month, island to island, demonstrated that the Japanese people, military and civilians, were ready to fight to the death. Often they readily committed suicide for the emperor. They weren't ready to surrender.

*An invasion would have cost tens of thousands of U.S. lives and probably over a million Japanese lives.

*The bombs provided a quick and surprising end to the war. It was so sudden that most Japanese POW camp commanders never had a chance to carry out their "kill them all" order, thus saving thousands of POWs from execution.

*The Soviets declared war on Japan in August and prepared to invade. If the war had continued, Japan would have ended up as a divided country like Germany. Over the decades, millions of Japanese would have disappeared to work/slave camps in Siberia and elsewhere in support of the Soviet empire – never to return.

*The horrors of Hiroshima and Nagasaki left indelible images for

Ken Bainbridge, left, and Robert Wilson toast each other with cups of ice water after being interviewed by the Smithsonian at GZ in 1988. Behind them is the Dave McDonald ranch house at base camp. The two men were important to the success of the test at Trinity but worked hard after the war to make sure nuclear weapons were under civilian control and were never used again. Like many of their comrades, they seemed proud of their scientific accomplishment, but regretted the bomb's use on Japan. WSMR photo.

decades following World War II. Because of those graphic photos and stories, so far, no world leader has been willing to "pull the trigger" on the use of nuclear weapons. President Truman fired the legendary General McArthur for proposing and publicly advocating their use against the Chinese in Korea. Without that Japanese example, McArthur might have gotten his way, and the result could have been a major exchange of nuclear weapons in Southeast Asia. Tens of millions of people would have died and huge areas may have been made uninhabitable.

*Finally, I heard one story about a British philanthropist who was invited to the annual Hiroshima memorial service. He was invited because of his humanitarian work around the world and in Japan after the war. I guess the assumption was that he would be very sympathetic to the organizer's cause. When he arrived, he was questioned by the Japanese news media. They asked what he thought about what the Americans had done to them at Hiroshima. The man took a second to consider the Japanese atrocities in China, Korea, the Philippines and Indochina. He then said, "I think you probably got what you asked for." He was immediately uninvited to the event and left standing on the airport tarmac.

Trinity Site's Future

Since 2010, Trinity Site has suffered with the downsizing of the military and cuts to the research budget. White Sands Missile Range, being at the end of the money pipeline, must make do with what trickles out after everyone upstream has taken what they want. Funds have been so tight, the missile range fell back to only hosting one Trinity open house a year. Officials simply didn't have the few dollars in the budget to pay for employee overtime and the necessary bus and portable toilet rentals.

With no money for four buses to run the shuttle service from the parking lot to the Schmidt/McDonald ranch, the house was recenlty dropped as a place to visit during the open houses. It probably was not a bad thing as the house has fallen into disrepair because there hasn't been any significant maintenance in years. At the end of 2014, missile range officials were expecting extra funds to conduct repairs at the house.

I think part of the problem is a disconnect between the big Army, as a huge organization, and Trinity Site. The feeling I have is that the Army doesn't "own" the site as part of its history. That is too bad because it was an Army Corps of Engineers project with a couple of Army generals running the show. The people like Marvin Davis, Carl Rudder, Felix DePaula and Loren Bourg were all young soldiers serving just like so many other men. Their immediate commander, Lieutenant Howard Bush went on to a full career in the Army.

Another aspect to the problem is the fact that Trinity Site belonged to Los Alamos which was run by the Army but not quite "the Army." Many regular Army folks viewed it as a freakish scientific research place that had little to do with real Army stuff like tanks and bazookas.

Of course, this was compounded when most all things nuclear fell under the newly created Atomic Energy Commission in 1947. Los Alamos and its associated sites were suddenly under civilian control. The ties were quickly cut and the Army was separated from its short adventure in developing atomic bombs.

Today, most of the nuclear weapons history in the U.S. is associated with places like Oak Ridge, Hanford and Los Alamos. Those sites belong to the Department of Energy, as the successor to the AEC, and most of the war development history falls to the DOE.

The DOE might be interested in helping with Trinity Site. So might the National Park Service as they were interested at day one. The Army would probably be happy to take unencumbered money from them to maintain the site but would certainly resist these outside agencies having anything to say about what happens on White Sands.

In the end, Trinity Site is one of the few WWII nuclear sites still under the Army's control but gets lost in the background noise. The Army acknowledges Trinity Site but it is almost just a footnote.

When I coordinated the Trinity Open Houses, I always dreamed of some real money upfront, maybe from a Congressional plus up, to add permanent improvements to accommodate visitors and cut down on the amount of required missile range support. Unfortunately, that is probably not a political reality for a site, no matter how important, that is only open to the public occasionally.

Trinity Site is certainly not going away but how the public gets there and what that experience will be is a bit uncertain at the beginning of 2015.

Additional Photos

Support personnel at Trinity relax with their own private swimming pool. This is the divided water storage tank just east of the Schmidt/McDonald ranch house as described by Frances Schmidt. No word on whether they used water hauled from Socorro or pumped it from the well which is next to the tank. Carl Rudder's scrapbook.

This is the building Marvin Davis says was dragged from an old mine in Mockingbird Gap to use as the "Blacksmith and Saddlers Shop." Carl Rudder's scrapbook.

This is the east side of base camp. At the left of the photo is a tent. The structure next to it is the Dave McDonald ranch house. The mountains in the background make up the north end of the San Andres range and are sometimes called the Mockingbirds. This photo and the one on the next page were taken the same day and from the same spot. Note the three vehicles on the right side of the photo. They show up in the same parking spots on the left side of the next photo so these images overlap a bit. Los Alamos photo.

This is the west side of base camp with the same three vehicles at the left edge that are in the east side photo. The barracks building just beyond the vehicles belonged to the military police. To the west of the barracks is a large T-shaped building with a cupola or vent on top that was the mess hall. White Sands Missile Range also had one of these mess halls installed erected on its main post in 1945. It served as the officers' mess. The building between the mess hall and the camera, with the flag pole to its side, was Ross McDonald's ranch house. Ross was Dave's partner in the ranch. The building right below the camera is one of the ranch barns. Los Alamos photo.

The work crew poses with their handiwork, a stack of 100 tons of TNT on a 20-foot platform made of heavy wooden timbers. The poles to the right and left of the platform are lightning arrestors. On May 7, 1945 it all disappeared when the stack was detonated. Since this explosion lacked the heat of an atomic bomb blast, many of the metal components to the tower survived. For instance, military policeman Marvin Davis found a large bent and twisted bolt from the tower. Los Alamos photo.

The top photo shows Jumbo arriving at its final location after being pulled and pushed from the Pope railroad siding. Note there is no tower yet but the concrete piers in the bottom of the pit have been poured. The bottom photo has Jumbo and its support frame being slid off the trailer and under the tower. The huge block and tackle hanging down will be used to raise Jumbo in the tower so the support materials can be removed. Los Alamos photos.

The two barrage balloons used to carry instruments aloft just west of the tower at GZ. Photography of the first moments of the explosion captures them being vaporized. Los Alamos photo.

This is the lead box setup devised by photographer Berlyn Brixner to protect the high-speed Fastax cameras at only 800 yards from the tower. To the right is the lead box with the mirrors mounted on top. In the middle, the cameras have been pulled out of the box for servicing. When pushed back in, the section with "255" on it is up against the lead box. Cables were attached to the sled this rests on so the recovery crew could stand well back after the test and pull the sled and cameras to them. Los Alamos photo.

These photos show N1,000 before and after the test. In the top photo, at the very right edge, the 100-foot test tower is visible. This bunker housed equipment to measure radiation. Because they didn't know what the magnitude would be, they ran several sets of instruments set to different levels hoping one would be right. The equipment got hot so the generators were necessary to run air conditioning equipment. Lead bricks for protecting equipment from radiation are stacked in the foreground. In the bottom photo, Jumbo can be seen in the background, right of center. Los Alamos photos.

This is the W10,000 photo bunker. On top there is what looks like a little dome. It is the gun mount below that has been transformed into a camera mount for a Mitchell 35mm movie camera. Julian Mack manned the camera during the test. The concrete portion to this bunker is still standing. The wooden backside, here in darker gray, has been removed. Los Alamos photos.

We always knew VIPs watched the test from the side of Compania Hill, some 20 miles northwest of GZ but were surprised at this. This image from the Los Alamos photos is labeled as "post shot view from distant station Compana Hill." The photo is taken looking toward Trinity Site. At the hazy top of the photo, just barely visible, is the dark line of the Oscura Mtns. with the Little Burros and Mockingbird Gap in the center and then the tail end of the San Andres Mtns. on the right.

Above is a formal portrait of Kenneth Bainbridge from Los Alamos. Below is a less formal portrait of Frances Schmidt Hall taken around 1913 or 1914. The photo of Frances was provided when she visited the old homestead one last time in 2003.

Captain C.L. Rutherford, pilot from the Iowa Civil Air Patrol who flew George Cremeens to Trinity Site poses by the GZ tower footings. Cremeens collection.

Sergeant Omer Loyd, left, is interviewed by George Cremeens of KRNT radio from Des Moines, Iowa. The interview took place in the base camp mess hall. Loyd was a military policeman. Cremeens collection.

Some of the support personnel at base camp. Captain Howard Bush is on the far right. See how many dogs you can count in this photo. Carl Rudder scrapbook.

A photo of the author opening the gate to Trinity Site appeared in this December 1980 issue of Playboy magazine in Japan.

125

Appendix A
Albert Einstein's Letter

Old Grove Rd.
Nassau Point
Peconic, Long Island

August 2nd, 1939
F.D. Roosevelt,
President of the United States,
White House
Washington, D.C.

Sir:

Some recent work by E. Fermi and L. Szilard, which has been communicated to me in manuscript, leads me to expect that the element uranium may be turned into a new and important source of energy in the immediate future. Certain aspects of the situation which has arisen seem to call for watchfulness and, if necessary, quick action on the part of the administration. I believe therefore that it is my duty to bring to your attention the following facts and recommendations:

In the course of the last four months it has been made probable -- through the work of Joliot in France as well as Fermi and Szilard in America -- that it may become possible to set up a nuclear chain reaction in a large mass of uranium, by which vast amounts of power and large quantities of new radium like elements would be generated. Now it appears almost certain that this could be achieved in the immediate future.

This new phenomenon would also lead to the construction of bombs, and it is conceivable -- though much less certain -- that extremely powerful bombs of a new type may thus be constructed. A single bomb of this type, carried by boat and exploded in a port, might very well destroy the whole port together with some of the surrounding territory. However, such bombs might very well prove to be too heavy for transportation by air.

The United States has only very poor ores of uranium in moderate quantities. There is some good ore in Canada and the former Czechoslovakia, while the most important source of Uranium is Belgian Congo.

continued on next page

In view of this situation you may think it desirable to have some permanent contact maintained between the Administration and the group of physicists working on chain reactions in America. One possible way of achieving this might be for you to entrust with this task a person who has your confidence and who could perhaps serve in an unofficial capacity. His task might comprise the following:

a) to approach Government Departments, keep them informed of the further development, and out forward recommendations for Government action, giving particular attention to the problem of uranium ore for the United States;

b) to speed up the experimental work, which is at present being carried on within the limits of the budgets of University laboratories, by providing funds, if such funds be required, through his contacts with private persons who are willing to make a contribution for this cause, and perhaps also by obtaining the co-operation of industrial laboratories which have the necessary equipment.

I understand that Germany has actually stopped the sale of uranium from the Czechoslovakian mines, which she has taken over. That she should have taken such early action might perhaps be understood on the ground that the son of the German Under-Secretary of State, von Weizäcker [sic], is attached to the Kaiser-Wilhelm-Institut in Berlin where some of the American work on uranium is now being repeated.

Yours very truly,

(Albert Einstein)

Appendix B
Schmidt Letters

AUTHOR'S NOTE: This is the first letter Public Affairs received from Frances Schmidt Hall. It was her father Franz who built the ranch house where the plutonium bomb core was assembled at Trinity Site. There is no date on the handwritten letter but it seems to me it arrived in 1986.

Dear Sirs,

We received the pictures of the McDonald Ranch at Trinity that you gave to Don McClenagan. We will never be able to thank you enough for them. You see, my father had that house built, I would say, the first part of 1913. My sister was born in July and was a small baby when we moved in -- it would have been in the fall -- Mama and I walked behind the wagon picking Black-eyed Susans (fall flowers).

You don't know how happy it makes me to know the place will be taken care of. Thank Mr. Fulwyler for us. Wish we could thank him in person.

The ranch will always be home to me -- to think of all that happened there -- July 16 is mama's birthday. The house was built by an old Norwegian stone mason daddy picked up off the streets and gave a home the rest of his life -- he is buried on a hill out there.

The painting and scroll work on the borders were done by a man from Chicago who came to N. Mex. dying with T.B. He lived with us and got strong and well. He also cared for the car – the first on the flats. That is why the garage and the grease pit – it made it easier to get under the car and turn down grease cups and things. It also was a fine place to play.

The barn was used mostly for shearing – wool sacks were nice to play on too if we didn't get caught.

The water tanks were for watering the sheep and a garden between the house and the yard fence. Believe it or not we had flowers in the yard -- zinnias all along the south wall that was my job to water.

In the house, the room used for assembly was mamas and daddys bedroom – mine was the smaller one. The other front room was the living room – then the kitchen and dining room opened to the back and the ice room with a pass through into a small room for keeping milk and things and the cellar underneath. What memories this all brings.

Daddy was a German boy that came to this country and mama was a farm girl from Texas and were only trying to make a home. His name was Franz Schmidt. He also had a brother here – he had a ranch on the flats west of Mocking Bird Gap – we owned that too. Wonder what happened to the well and tank there – there was a small wooden house there – it had been a post office called Murry at one time.

North of the ranch we had another house built by the same old man at Hansonburg Hills – old John was living there when he died.

We can't thank you enough for the pictures and restoring the place.

Wonder what happened to a big rock on the mountain in front of the house? It was a big shaft of red or pink granite sticking straight up out of the side of the mountain.

My daughter had written a more complete letter – but I just wanted to thank all of you – we didn't have pictures of that home as we didn't have a camera at that time. Later we have some pictures of the place at Hansonburg.

Thanks all of you again.

Frances Hall

AUTHOR'S NOTE: *This detailed letter was written in 1986 and signed by Rosemary Hall, the daughter of Frances Schmidt Hall. When I met the family, they indicated Rosemary was recording her mother's information for her.*

Dear Sir:

The house at Trinity Site was built between late 1912 & early 1913. My Grandfather & Grandmother moved into it around August or September of 1913. The house was adobe with pebble-dash outside walls. The inside walls were smooth plaster. Floors were of wood. In the front were concrete half circle steps. The roof was tin with 18" anchor bolts into the adobe walls. This was because of the high winds & to prevent it from being pulled off. The north side of the house had a filter with charcoal to purify the water from the roof, as it went into the cistern for storage. The cellar was part ice house. Ice was cut from the water tanks during the winter. At this time there was no electricity or plumbing, only an outhouse. This was located at the rear of the housed marked "root cellar."

The Ice House area was joined to the house by an open breezeway, roofed but no doors on either end. The steps were half circle also. There was a cellar located under the ice house.

The kitchen/dining room was painted pale gray. This is in the right place. There was a Magic Chef wood range for cooking.

The "southeast room" was the living room. It was either tan or a pink/peach color.

The "assembly room" was my grandparents bedroom. It was pale green.

The "northwest room" was my mother's room. It was blue. The two younger children slept in my grandparent's room because one was ill at times & one a baby.

The living room had a stove in the style of a pot belly stove. It had an eisenglass door & a chrome rail at the bottom. You could prop your feet up on this.

There were 2 kerosene lamps in the kitchen with reflectors for light. Other lamps were silver colored with green glass shades, also a rayovac lamp that used a mantel (wick). The pot belly stove had a chrome knob on top.

My mother doesn't remember the trap doors in the "northwest room" or in the kitchen. There were young cottonwood trees in a row on the front of the house. a zinnia bed was at the south side of the house. A garden was between the house & the water tanks. (you call this a reservoir). The garden was watered from the water tank. There were two valves on the water tank, one for the garden & one on the opposite side for the sheep water trough.

The windmill at the water tank was where my grandmother hung meat wrapped in a sheet. This was before the ice house was finished. Animals couldn't get to the meat there.

The bunkhouse was a small tool/tack room, a room for my grandfather's brother Frank Holmes & Mr. John Finago (not sure of the spelling). The room on the back of it was a storeroom for groceries & other supplies.

The barn & garage was a garage with work pit & the room at the end of the garage belonged to Mike Walsh. The barn was for shearing sheep & stacking of wool bags. There was also a hack & a wagon. The bunkhouse & barn also had tin roofs. These were to catch rainwater because water was scarce. Snow was also used to fill the cisterns.

The long water trough was for sheep & the short one for horses.

The driveway was on the south side of the house, so you could leave the car at the garage.

The ceilings in the house were cream color with drop ceiling (drop 18" from ceiling in same cream color). The ceiling color & main wall color were divided by a stencil scroll border. The main scroll was in the corners. This was done by Mike Walsh. He was from Chicago & was buried in Albuquerque, N. Mexico by my grandparents. He had care of the care & drove it, among other jobs at the ranch.

John Finago was a Norwegian stone mason who did the fence & other stone work here & the Hansonburg Hills house. This was also part of the ranch, as was Mockingbird Gap. The grave of John Finago is on a hill close to the house.

The adobe used for the house was made right next to the house. We guess the pit was filled in over the years. The windows were eight pane glass.

The original homestead & house was one mile down range. It was burned when my grandmother was in town for the arrival of her second baby. The family lived in the barn there with a fireplace for cooking. This was added on. The house at Trinity Site was then built. There were two large storage tanks for filling the concrete dipping vat at the homestead site. Also, a well & pump.

Four wagons of groceries & supplies were brought to the ranch twice a year. Jean Val Jean owned the freight line that delivered them. He was from San Marcial, N. Mexico. Two wagons were hooked together & pulled by six mules.

Wood for heating & cooking was cut in the mountains & hauled to the ranch by wagon. The woodpile was at the water tank.

This was a working ranch of over 12,000 head of sheep. Six herds of 2,000 plus sheep were worked. Each had a herder & usually a dog. One was a Scotsman called George & his dog Mary. The wool was sold in New York. The buyers came at shearing time to the ranch or sometimes in town.

Over 1,000 cattle were here also. My grandfather brought the first two purebred bulls to New Mexico. One was a Shorthorn & the other a Roan Shorthorn or white face Hereford. The cows were common Chihuahua cattle.

The first car was here at the ranch. It was a Dodge (1913 or 1914).

At the barns was a sheep gate. You could lift the lower part for sheep to come through but not the horses. They watered at the long trough in the corral. This was at the home ranch (Trinity Site).

The ranch was sold because of my grandfather's health beginning to fail. It was sold to a Mr. Synder then later on to McDonald. I don't know if the name can be changed but in reality, my grandparents were the original owners & builders. Some was homesteaded & a part of it bought. This should show on the old records. It should be called the Schmidt Ranch. It was still the Territory of New Mexico at this time.

My grandfather came through Ellis Island at the age of 17. He was born Franz Schmidt in Julich, Rhein Prussia (now Germany). He became an American citizen. My grandmother was Esther Holmes from Pearsall, Texas. They were married in 1906 & had three children. Frances (my mother), Thomas & Margaret.

I hope this helps some. My mother is so proud you cared enough to preserve & restore her home. You will never know how much the picture

& information you sent, means to here. If you want to talk to her in person, we are only about 50 miles north of Eglin Air Force Base. Enclosed is some information related to the area & some pictures. Any questions, just ask. As a matter of trivia, the bomb was tested on my grandmother's birthday.

Could you provide some information on a red granite (?) shaft? When you stood at the front door (at Trinity Site) it was straight ahead on the mountain side. It looked similar to the Washington Monument but flat on top. People that looked down on it said the top might have a hollow because it held water after a rain. It could not be climbed because it was straight & slick. (Author's Note: We never saw this shaft)

There was also a rock house built at Hansonburg Hills at the same time or just after the house at Trinity Site. It was also built by John Finago, same design, but smaller & no ice house. It was used mainly as a bunkhouse by my grandfather & John Finago or whatever crew was working the stock. This was about six miles from the home ranch. There were two metal tanks for water plus the earth water tank.

At Mockingbird Gap there was a wood house, one room frame, used as a home for my great-grandmother. Prior to this, before 1900, it was a post office called Murray (?) officially listed as a Post Office. Messages & mail were left & people checked for mail as they rode by. Sometimes delivering mail to people if they were going that way. There was a steel windmill that pumped water into a large earth tank. There should have been a spring here because the wagon trains crossed here in the 1800s. If they didn't get water here, they were in trouble because of the distance to the next water. The Indians plugged all the springs in the mountains with rocks & cedar bark. The trains could be ambushed before reaching the Gap. On the south side hubs from burned trains could be seen on the prairie when my mother was a child. It was thirty five miles to the river for the next water, for example, depending on which way they were headed.

Sincerely,
Rosemary A. Hall

Appendix C
Marvin Davis Sr. Letters

AUTHOR'S NOTE: In the mid 80s, military policeman Marvin Davis wrote the Public Affairs Office a string of letters recounting life at Trinity Site and Los Alamos. Also, he brought his family out to reunions at Los Alamos and some of the Trinity Site open houses. Most of these are entire letters but in a few cases I've selected the most pertinent sections to reproduce. He was pretty good at dating his letters so I've tried to arrange everything in chronological order. Davis died on Oct. 22, 2009.

FEBRUARY 11, 1983

I am sending you a few of the pictures I still have, taken during 1945. I hope they might be of some interest to you. I put a few notations on the backs of the pictures along with my original notes. There are quite a few pictures of the horses, for we were a mounted outfit (one of the last). Major Bush came from the old 101st Cavalry out of Ft. Devon, Mass. Most of our original group came from the Military Police Replacement Center at Ft. Riley, Kan. and the Mounted Group went to Cavalry School there. We got to Los Alamos in April of 1943 and took over the security there. I doubt if there were over 250 people on the "Hill" at that time. But oh how it grew. Major Bush was given the job of selecting the men and going to Trinity to start the patrol and security of the Range. Of course he took his mounted group, except for a man to do the cooking. I think he was an old drunk the Major saved from the Stockade, but he really could cook, as long as he had a little nip once in a while, and we tried to keep him supplied when we went on a convoy to Las Alamos.

I don't know if the trailer still exists that brought Jumbo to the site from the Pope railroad siding over to the west side of the Range. They built a building to put it in to keep it out of sight. It had 8 rows of wheels with 8 in each row. Like a motor grader's wheels.

I got ahead of my story, we came down to the Range Dec. 30, 1944 and most of the original men started to be eligible for discharge during the winter of 1945. I was discharged in Feb. of 1946 since I was a little younger than some of the men. I had some pictures I sent to the Los Alamos Historical Society Museum. I was at the 30th Reunion at Los Alamos in 1975.

What got me interested in Dave McDonald was, while I was at the Reunion, an English T.V. producer was making a documentary for BBC and interviewed me and a buddy who were the only security men there. He had already talked to McDonald and that he had accused us of killing his cattle. This T.V. man really tried to get some information out of us, so we kind of lost our memory. I do feel a little guilty when I see the Golden Arches.

In the evenings we played a lot of volleyball – we had the net stretched between the latrine and our barracks. I wonder what people would think of volleyball teams with names like Enrico Fermi, George Kistiakowski, Norris Bradbury on them. They were all glad to relax in the evening and get their minds off their work.

I could write a book on the things that happened and what we did down there. I guess I'll quit now before I have a novel written here. I hope you can use the pictures and what information I have given. Now, I remember something else. I still have the last film badge I wore – they were to register any radiation we absorbed, also the arc welders glass that I watched the Test through. I was told to look at an oblique angle instead of straight at it. We had them taped in a cardboard shield. I still couldn't keep my eyes open and the heat was like opening up an over door, even at 10 miles. I often wonder if any of the men suffered from radiation. I don't think I had any effects, but all I did was to take the men to their posts when the guards were posted, I didn't stay too long around Zero Point.

AUTHOR'S NOTE: Davis lived a long and full life. He died on Oct. 22, 2009 at the age of 87. As for his film badge, he donated it to Public Affairs. We sent it to Los Alamos to learn more about it. This is the lab's response:

"The film badge, returned for inspection and identification, was specially prepared for the Trinity test. One hundred such badges were prepared, and some were issued to personnel for the Trinity test. Our records indicate that this particular badge and many others of this same type were never returned for evaluation, suggesting that this badge was a spare, unused badge. According to our records:

100 Special Autopsy Type: containing Eastman type K and DuPont 12 D-1 films and Adlux paper packs (for high range – 100 to 1,500). On the outside of the badge is taped a #4 capsule of red phosphorus for neutron measurements. These badges are identified by a red band on the top of the badge. These also have neck bands for facility in wearing. They come packed three in a box.....

The film labeled "REGULAR K" SAFETY FILM was the Eastman type K film, which was capable of measuring exposures from 0 to 7R. The film with the green tab contained the DuPont 12-D-1 and Adlux films. The DuPont 12-D-1 film had a sensitivity from about 0.1 to 100R. The Adlux film had a sensitivity indicated above, from 100 to 1500R.

The corrosion on the front of the badge is probably due to chemical reactions of the red phosphorus and air with the brass, after the capsule was broken."

When the White Sands Missile Range Museum was established, the film badge and other Davis materials were on display in its "Trinity" room. As all artifacts in the Army Museum system technically belong to the Army's Center for Military History, that organization snatched the badge some time ago and it is no longer in New Mexico.

MAY 30, 1983

I am starting this, though I don't know when I will get it finished. As I told you we came from Ft. Riley, Kansas. They took us down through Texas, the cooks and company people got off at Ft. Worth and went directly to Los Alamos, the rest ended up at Camp Wolters, Tex. The mounted group that I was in stayed two days and the rest came about two weeks later.

They took us on a scenic tour, through Texas and then up through New Mexico to Lamy, and then the troop train was switched back up into Santa Fe. We were unloaded, out by the old prison and put onto buses and trucks and taken up to Los Alamos. "The Hill." If I remember correctly it was April 19, 1943. The buses and trucks couldn't make those hairpin turns on the old road, so they had to jockey back and forth to get around them, which wasn't too pleasing to a "Flatland Furriner" like me, though I've learned to love the mountains since, and have traveled out there quite a bit.

There were very few people on the "Hill" at that time, mostly construction people. On fatigue duty, we had to haul furniture from the warehouse around to the civilian houses and apartments, and later we had to saw wood for them. We also dug ice out of the old "Ice House" by the old water tower at Ashley Pond to be taken around to the apartments.

The only horses and equipment we had was the stuff that came with the Ranch School when the government bought it. We didn't even have any weapons at first, only the officers and non-coms had side arms. My first guard duty was riding around the Tech Area on one of these ranch horses and my only weapon was a M.P.'s nightstick. When I used my flashlight to check the locked gates the old horse threw me over his head, I landed on the back of my neck and shoulders in the dust. We were so short on people we worked a lot of 8 hour shifts, and riding a horse for 8 hours around the post sure gets to be a drag. They would bring a relief for us to eat and use the latrine. After they got more personnel in, where it was possible, we worked shorter shifts.

I don't know who was responsible for the purchase but they brought in a bunch of green broken western horses, that came from over around Las Vegas, N.M. Boy, did we have a rodeo checking those horses out. We had to learn to rope them and tie them up short to saddle them up. The roping came in handy when we became "amateur cowboys" later. We got a nice bunch of re-mounts from El Reno, Oklahoma later. I think we had 16 of them at Trinity.

The picture on page 33 in the booklet, Los Alamos 1943-1945, is the shelter we built for the horses and the building we skidded from the old mine in Mockingbird Gap, to be used as a black smith shop. The shelter had solid ends and back with tarps over the top. We stored our hay in the old adobe buildings in the foreground of the camp photo on page 34 of the booklet. Our barracks was the one nearest the Mess Hall with the Orderly Room at the near end.

I helped pull the push rods and some of the casing on the windmill in the foreground, we tried to increase the flow but it didn't succeed too well. We used a winch on a 4x4 truck to pull the casing – we rigged a pulley on the ground and one up the windmill tower to pull the casing out of the ground. We put new casings and a new ball valve in the well.

The engineers hadn't arrived yet so Sgt. Barnett and I got a bulldozer started and dug out our first garbage pit – he operated the dozer and I manipulated the blade. There were a few stalls, but we got it done.

The picture on page 35 in the booklet must have been taken on the other windmill tower. That well had been started but it must have caved in. It was a larger diameter casing than the old well. They put a well drilling outfit from Ft. Sumner to work opening it up, and they went down over 400 feet hoping to get below the deposit of gypsum in the valley but the water was still alkali.

Captain Davalos, the Engineer Officer, tried putting a water softener in but the water was just too alkaline. We hauled our drinking water from the Fire House in Socorro. We all carried water bags on our vehicles. The water stayed cool in spite of the heat.

We got our gasoline from the Standard bulk plant in Socorro owned by Mrs. Mary Apodaca. We got pretty well acquainted with her and her family – also the soda bottler and beer distributor in Socorro. I think their name was Hammel, Clarence and Marcella.

After we started getting our mail at Box 632 Socorro, we could make the mail run and get a haircut at the shop in town. Sometimes we got so shaggy, we had to use the horse clippers to trim our hair up and they were about a foot long with a head about 4 inches wide, but Sgt. Greyshock could do a pretty decent job with them.

In the booklet they talk about getting antelope steak in the Mess Hall, but we didn't get too many antelope after we tried the first one or two. We did get quite a few of the big mule deer though, and they were really good eating. We had one cook that could really fix those venison steaks and chops, so they could be cut with a fork. The white faces weren't too bad either, but like I said before I still feel guilty when I go into a MacDonald's hamburger stand.

After I told some the fellows I worked with about the things we did, one of them started calling me the "Old Rustler" and it struck with me. Now my C.B. handle is "Rustler."

Most of the references to Major Bush are, as a lieut. but I think he was a Captain when we came and made Major after the test when about everyone jumped a rank. I know he went to Ft. Bliss to take the test for his permanent Captaincy, later in 1945. He was a real diplomat, but he could get tough when he had to. He did everything he could to make things easier for everyone, military and civilians alike.

I don't know how or where he got it, but got some polo equipment for us and we used to play out past the motor pool. We had the regulation helmets, mallets and the wooden balls although I think we had as much fun playing with a soccer ball and old brooms, that we cut part of the straw off of the bottom.

Major Bush let us use the Army carbines to hunt the deer with but he was kind of selective as to who he let use them. Sometimes if he wasn't too sure about some one, he would have one of us non-coms go with him. Like I said before, there were not many antelope killed and there were still thousands left there on the range when I was discharged in Feb. 1946. We used the Army ammunition but we took a rasp and filed the bronze off the tips of the bullets so the lead was exposed and then the bullet would expand more.

He tried to give us a 30 day leave in August and September of 1945, but they were only given to overseas returnees at that time. So he talked them into giving us a 15 day leave with travel time and then he told us to wire for a 10 day extension and he would grant it, and that any kind of excuse would do. When I was on as duty Sgt. in the Orderly Room we were reading some of the telegrams and laughing at some of the excuses. I'll never forget the one that said, "Request ten days extension to get married, and to care of some urgent personal business." This fellow married one of the W.A.C.s from the Hill – I still write to him once in a while.

Major Bush invited about 20 or 25 W.A.C.s down for Christmas of 45 and we had quite a blowout. We had a couple kegs of beer and 3 or 4 cases of booze. Most of the W.A.C.s were wilder than the antelope though.

When I went to the reunion at Los Alamos in 1975, they told me they had contacted Bush for the 1970 reunion and that he was at the Redstone Arsenal in Huntsville, Alabama and was a Colonel.

There were a lot of funny things that happened, one was a mustache contest that Pfc. Joe Reed won – he beat Bush out by two inches. His, when it was waxed was nine inches from tip to tip. Then there was a fellow from New York City that had never seen popcorn popped. I had an aunt and uncle that were farmers and raised popcorn and they sent me some un-popped corn. So we went to the Mess Hall and popped some and this fellow really got a kick out of it, so I gave it all to him.

Another time one of the weather men came running into the Orderly Room asking for a gun, to kill a big rattlesnake they had cornered under a pile of plywood. Bush told him he wasn't going to let him shoot up the camp, so we all got a stick of wood and went over and kind of gingerly moved the plywood and I could see it was a big bull snake, that is harmless, so I put my 2x4 on his neck and caught him – and carried him over by the Rec Hall. He might as well have been a rattler because everyone scattered like a bunch of quail. It's a wonder we didn't have any snake bites, for there was really a lot of them. I only saw one really large one, and I think it was a diamondback. I killed it over by the watch tower in Mockingbird Gap. We saw a lot of scorpions, they liked the latrine, so we had to check around the corners and under the seats before we sat down.

Bush had the little wire haired terrier and it tangled with a porcupine under a barracks and came out on the short end of it. The Medic was Si Lernor of Beloit, Wisc. and he gave the little dog ether and pulled and cut the quills out, but little dog was never the same after that. I think some of the points were still in him and they would work out and cause a sore on his neck and shoulders. And he couldn't move his head too well after that.

If I saw the rattlesnakes on the road I always tried to run over them. and if you hit them just right they would pop like a paper bag.

One of the first times we found a scorpion was on a roadblock out at the crossroads. When I drove up to check the post the young fellow on guard told me he had seen a crawdad and was wondering why it was so far from water. I asked him if he had tried to pick it up and he said he hadn't. So I told him don't ever try it because they might not kill you but they hurt so bad you'll wish you were dead.

I was really surprised at the amount of wildlife out on the range. In fact, I got a young hawk out of a nest in a yucca before he was feathered out and I raised him to full growth. We would kill one or two jackrabbits almost every shift so I would bring one in to him and he would really make the fur fly. Sometimes I'd get a piece of meat from the Mess Hall for him. I finally turned him loose and he stayed around camp for a while. He would land on the telephone pole that we had for a flag pole and wait for a piece of meat and he would swoop down to get it and then go up on one of the windmill towers to eat it.

We had the usual run of dogs that seem to appear at Army camps. The young collie that is in the one picture I sent, came from one of the sheep ranches over west of camp. I sent him home in January of 1946 and he became one of the most beautiful collies I've ever seen, and with out any training he was one of the most intelligent dogs I've seen. My oldest son and some of my nephews, about the same age, really had a time with him – pulling a sled for them. I had him till he was fourteen, but he got so crippled up and sick I had to have him put to sleep. He was an out-door dog I that I could hardly get to come into the house. Even as a pup he would curl up in a ball along side of the barracks and the snow would cover him up, and thats where he would sleep. When I first got him, I thought he was deaf, but I found after checking his ears they were full of sheep ticks and were infected so I got a pair of tweezers from the Vet supplies and pulled them out and then poured peroxide into his ears and it really took care of the infection.

You might think I have been tooting my horn, but I imagine some of the other fellows would have memories of other things that happened. I came from a family that grew up during the 30s when times were pretty tough and we all worked together to make a living. My folks always told us to not say "I can't" and to say "I'll try." You would be surprised how many "can't do" things turn into "can do's."

I've been trying to get this written for over three weeks, but I've been building a deck on the back of our house besides keeping about an acre of grass mowed.

P.S. These are some of the original twelve men.

1st Sgt. Richard O'Meara – West Hartford, Conn.
T. Sgt. Sam H. Barnett – Houston, Tex.
T. Sgt. Carl Dirksen – Ft. Pierre, S.D.
T. Sgt. Reno Moses – N.C.
Sgt. Amer Loyd – Indianapolis, Ind.
Sgt. Dan Shotel – Philadelphia, Penn.
Sgt. Marvin Davis – Bartonville, Ill.
Sgt. Dillard Maher (Blacksmith) – W. Va.
Cpl. Rex Harris – Idaho Falls, Ida.
Cpl. Richard Coleman – Roanoke, Virg.
Pfc. Fechner – N.J.

I really didn't explain all of my duties while at Trinity. We were divided into 3 guard sections. Sgt. Barnett and I had one, Sgt. Moses and Sgt. Loyd another and Sgt. Dirksen and Sgt. Shotel the other.

We worked 12 hour shifts, one week of days and one of nights and one week off during which we pulled the details that had to be done around camp. Some 3 day passes were given later and some of the married fellows went to Albuquerque or Santa Fe to be with their wives. On a pass they had to go there because they didn't want us to spend any time south of Albuquerque.

The sergeants divided the shifts into 6 hours each. We took our men out to the posts and brought the ones that were on duty back to camp. We had one of those plywood hutments at the crossroads where the road from Mockingbird Gap came in and one of us stayed there while the other checked the posts for six hours. We tried to bring the men in to eat but we finally gave that up because of the distances and the horrible conditions of the roads. Because of the alkali dust the fellows couldn't hardly breathe in the back of those vehicles.

I don't know how it started but the fellows started cooking bacon and eggs on a hot plate or on the little stoves in cold weather and having peanut butter and jelly or marmalade for their meals and it worked out really well. It sure simplified things. Generally though, I cooked up a stew or soup in cold weather when I was on the 6 hour break. A stew was about the only thing you could make out of the antelope meat that was half way decent. I also made potato soup for me and Sgt. Barnett in the winter time. It is still one of my specialties.

I learned to make vegetable soup from one of the cooks there and I can't remember his name. He would take the bones from a quarter of beef and put them in one of those big 35 gallon pots and put it on the back burner and would cut up a stalk of celery and some onions in it and then let it simmer for a couple of days and then he would take the bones out and add the vegetables to it and that made some of the best vegetable soup I ever ate. We had a regular Mess Hall crew so none of our men had to do any of the Mess Hall details.

On our week off we tried to keep everything cleaned up and presentable. About the time we got the barracks all cleaned up, a dust devil would come through and we would have to do it over again. The glass in the windows was so sandblasted you couldn't hardly see through them or clean them. We couldn't keep everything ship shape because there was always some of the night shift sleeping during the day. To keep from disturbing them the stable crew partitioned the south end of the barracks off and made their own quarters there.

It is another hot, humid day here, the temperature is already over 90 degrees. Maybe I can think of something else later.

SEPTEMBER 8, 1983

AUTHOR'S NOTE: This letter from Davis is in response to some questions we posed to him about trespassers and the famous bombing incident when a practice bomb was dropped on the camp by a lost crew flying out of the Alamogordo Bombing Range.

We didn't have too much trouble with people trying to come into the range. A couple of time off-duty men from the air base tried to come up through the Gap but we spotted them right away. One time a rancher rode a horse right into base camp from the southwest, but I think he was just checking for cattle. That was kind of an open area, because we didn't have any guards in that direction or didn't patrol too often in that area either.

I don't really remember what I was doing when the Camp was bombed. I could have been watching one of those old films we were sent. I do remember some of the Engineers piling out of their barracks and hitting the ground – they were veterans of some of the campaigns in the South Pacific and had been through some rough times. According to the booklet you sent, a bomb hit the stable area but I don't remember any hitting there. As far as I know they hit in the Motor Pool area which was a little dangerous. They could have caused some damage if they had hit a vehicle or the gas tanks.

They were starting to fence in the crater area before I left but as far as filling it in, I don't know. I wouldn't say it was a crater, only a depression. As I remember the tower was on a slight rise and after the blast it was a saucer-like depression.

Things were still pretty hectic into August and September and then it quieted down and got more relaxed. As I told you before we worked one week of days and one week of nights and then we were off a week. The guard section that was off had the details around the Camp which didn't amount to much. Major Bush got permission to give passes on that off week, but we had to go to Albuquerque or Santa Fe. I was trying to save my money at that time so I didn't go on too many passes. So I let Sgt. Barnett have my passes since his wife was in Santa Fe. That was one reason I did a lot around the Camp. Also, I was the junior non-com in the horse outfit and was left with a lot of details when the senior non-coms were gone - such as going in to Socorro after the mail, or getting a tank truck of drinking water or gasoline.

The engineers drove the trucks, but sometimes they were busy grading the roads or on a convoy to Los Alamos, so we drove the short hauls.

I went hunting with some of the fellows sometimes and explored some of the old ranch sites. Its a wonder I never got snake bit. We went over to the old ghost town of Val Verde a few times, it was over near the Rio Grande. That's where a battle was fought in the Civil War.

I took a lot of pictures before I got out, and I left the film with a fellow in the photography outfit who said he would develop them and send them to me but that was the last I saw them. He must have kept them for himself.

SUNDAY, SEPTEMBER 1, 1985

Hi Jim,

I was glad to hear from you again and to receive the Anniversary copy of the Ranger. You must have had quite a Reunion according to the paper. We were at the Reunion at Los Alamos on June 14-15 & 16. We really had a good time. I met several fellows I hadn't seen since 45. I sure would have loved to have been down there in July for your Reunion but the money only goes so far.

I had an experience this summer on the anniversary of the Bomb Test. I offered one of the local TV newsmen the use of some of the pictures I had, for a newscast that evening, but he insisted on coming out to the house to interview me. I didn't want that especially but I relented and let him tape an interview, so I was on the evening news that night.

The next day I got a phone call from a fellow that had been up at Los Alamos with us, but he never came down to Trinity. He had worked at the Caterpillar Plant here 30 years and he just lives across the river from me about 6 or 8 miles and we had never crossed paths. He was originally from Arkansas but came up to go to work for the Cat.

I have decided to start writing a few letters to some of the fellows but most of the addresses I have are old. I have had good luck on a couple but one was returned and no answer on another. This one fellow took quite a few pictures so maybe I can induce him to share them. I'm not really sure but I think he is the one that saw the crawdads(scorpions). They usually send a booklet on the Reunion with pictures and addresses in it. If they do I might have a few more letters to write.

I think some of those Engineers in Rudder's picture, in your paper, are on the group picture I sent you. They didn't build the base, though, they put up a lot of those 18 ft. square hutment buildings and took care of the roads, but the old barracks and bunkers were there when we got there Dec. 30, 1944. The Engineers didn't get there till some time later. In fact Sgt. Sam Barnett and I got a bulldozer going and between the two of us dug the first garbage pit. He ran the dozer and I operated the blade. We stalled quite a few times, but we got it done.

The picture in the paper that is called the stables is the Blacksmith and Saddler's Shop. That's the old building we got at the old abandoned mine over in Mockingbird Gap. We put it on skids and drug it over to Base Camp. The shelter we built for the horses is pictured in the booklet *Los Alamos 1943-1945*, but the caption under it is wrong, too. I hope I can get some of those fellows that I write to, to give you some information and some pictures.

Thanks for the pictures last year and the copy of the Ranger. Will try to get you more information.

Marvin R. Davis Sr.

Appendix D
Carl Rudder Letters

AUTHOR'S NOTE: Carl Rudder didn't write much about his experiences at Trinity Site – maybe he simply let his scrapbook do the talking. Below is Carl's most informative letter to us. Also, I've included Loren Bourg's letter to Carl's wife in this section. It is a thank you for the Christmas card she sent him (probably at Carl's suggestion) and, I imagine, his way of sending card in return. Carl sent it to us because Bourg talks about life at the Camp. Like all these other letters, Bourg's is hand written but in the neatest penmanship we'd seen in a long time.

AUGUST 8, 1984

Dear Sir:

Thank you for your information on Trinity Site. I have started out there 3 times and still haven't made it. Hopefully this time I will.

You asked what my duties were. As I was a power lineman for the gov't (T.V.A.) I volunteered for a special assignment under the impression that I was going to Oak Ridge which was near my home. I was inducted on Jan. 26, past through 4 camps, took 2 days of basic and arrived at Trinity on or about Feb. 17, where I immediately became supervisor of what I named the "East Jesus and Socorro Light and Water Co." One man operation "ME" – I maintained 5 generators, 3 wells, and 5 pumps and did the line work.

Other than being gone from home, I really enjoyed my tour of duty. Especially the last 6 or 8 months when I was 2nd in command of Camp. I had a ball.

Enclosed are a few pictures that I have left, maybe you can use 1 or 2 of them. Over the years they have a way of disappearing.
Hoping to be there Oct. 6, I remain,

Carl A. Rudder

DECEMBER 22, 1945

Dear Mrs. Rudder:

I hardly now how to begin this letter, so I will make an attempt. I do hope you are not offended. First I want you to know that I appreciate the Christmas card, and I thank you very much.

Mrs. Rudder, I don't know just what Carl told you about me, but if you can bear with me I'll try and tell you more about myself. I am a boy from Houma, Louisiana. Before entering the Army I was in the fire department in my hometown.

Now to tell you how I was given the title of "chief." Upon entering the Army I was in the military police in Camp Polk, Louisiana. In April 1943 I was transferred to a German prisioner of war camp just out of Alva, Oklahoma, then in Sept. 1943, I was sent to Fort Bliss, Texas to be reassigned to a fire fighting unit going overseas.

Well, I joined my unit, but we ended up in Los Alamos above Santa Fe, N.M. Upon arrival there I was assigned as Station Sergeant working under the fire chief. In April of this year I was sent down here to take over the fire prevention and fire dept. Upon arrival I found I was the fire department, period. I was assigned as fire chief and safety officer. I met Carl, he was the first soldier I met here. I am very fond of him and consider him my best friend. Honest, I would do anything for him.

Carl and I just came in from a fire call. Upon arrival at the scene, we found that it was an overheated coal heater. The soot burnt out in the pipe, causing the pipe through the roof to turn white hot.

Oh, I forgot something; I came into the Army in November of 42. This is my fourth Christmas to be celebrated in an Army post. Every Christmas day so far, I had to work. This Christmas eve night I will be in charge of quarters. That means no sleep. So Christmas day I will be asleep, I hope.

Well Mrs. Rudder, I want to wish you, and yours a very Merry Christmas, and a real Happy New Year.
Yours Sincerely

Sgt. Loren R. Bourg

P.S. This is the first time I was ever real home sick on Christmas.

Appendix E
George Cremeens Documents

AUTHOR'S NOTE: This is the script George Cremeens used in his appearances in Iowa and Nebraska when he gave talks about his trip to Trinity Site in September 1945 to conduct his radio interviews. Usually he would provide this background information, play some of the recordings he made in New Mexico and then answer questions. Given what we know today, this account contains very little information about the test but does give us a feeling for the times.

There are numerous errors, like the time of the explosion and distances between places, which I have not corrected.

Thank you, Mr. _____. It was my good fortune to have the opportunity of covering for radio one of the outstanding news stories of our time. Up to this date, as far as I know, there have only been approximately fifteen men cleared by the War Department to view the test site of the world's first Atomic Bomb.

The first step in covering a story such as this is to get the proper clearances from the Bureau of Public Relations, War Department, Washington, D. C. From the Bureau of Creditation, a part of the Bureau of Public Relations, the final clearance is given.

Having received clearance for myself, our sound engineer, and our pilot, we took off from the Des Moines Airport at seven a. m. the morning of September 15th and flew directly to Kirtland Field, Albuquerque, New Mexico. The total flying time was six hours and thirty-five minutes.

After arriving at Albuquerque, it required two days of work to get the programs set up and arrangements made for the transcribing of the programs. The first program, in a series of four which I transcribed while at the scene, was made on a wire recorder while flying at 1500 feet over the crater. To make this broadcast, we took off from Albuquerque, New Mexico and flew south down the Rio Grande Valley.

We had a slight misfortune on this phase of our trip. Our total flying time from Albuquerque to the crater was to be sixteen minutes. We were to fly six minutes south and then take an east bearing from a town on the river and fly ten minutes. However, we flew for twelve minutes and couldn't find the town.

We continued flying south finally arriving at Hot Springs, New

Mexico and flew over the town then headed back toward Albuquerque. We sited what looked as if it might have been a town, took up an east bearing from that and after twenty minutes searching for the crater, we finally found it.

The crater, as you approach it, looks somewhat like a lake because of the green, crystalized sand around the crater itself. The terrain, at the point of the crater, is approximately 5500 feet above sea level. We were flying at an indicated altitude of 1500 feet above the ground.

To make the broadcast from the plane as audible as possible, I instructed the pilot to start at 1500 feet, throttle back his engine, and circle the crater -- thus, cutting to a minimum the noise of the motor. He had difficulty in maintaining safe flight because of the rarity of the air at that altitude.

We figured that we could safely circle for six minutes without getting too close to the earth so to make the fifteen minute show it was necessary for us to transcribe the program in sections. After cutting the first section, we climbed to fifteen hundred feet again and transcribed the second.

Such blasts as occurred in New Mexico during the test -- and at Nagasaki and Hiroshima -- never occurred on the earth before. After seeing the crater I, for one, heartily back up that statement.

As we circled the crater, the greenish sand seemed to change hue from green to blue and sparkled somewhat like small diamonds in the sunlight. The green surface is 400 to 500 yards around the crater. The crater, itself, is about 70 to 80 feet across. Unlike a crater created by TNT, which scoops out the earth, the Atomic Bomb blew the earth in. In other words, it compressed the earth into a saucer shape. To do this, pressure up to the thousands of pounds per square inch was necessary.

The only building we could see in the vicinity was an old ranch house some six miles distant from the crater. We could see from the air the road used by the Army to set up the necessary equipment for the test.

The crater is located in what is known as Oscura Basin, which was known to the early settlers as the "Journey of Death" because of the lack of water in the area.

The crater is circled on all sides by mountains which tower some eight to nine thousand feet. Surrounding area is spotted by small geysers, bubbling hot springs, and is the roughest terrain I have ever seen. Was spotted in different places with lava flows. If we had had motor trouble over this area, it would have been impossible to land.

After completing our broadcast, which you will hear a portion of later, we returned to Socorro, New Mexico and there we were met by Dr. K. T. Bainbridge, scientist in charge of selecting the site and setting up necessary arrangements for the detonation of the world's first Atomic Bomb. Dr. Bainbridge and Mr. Anderson, Public Relations Officer on the site, then

150

drove us forty-five miles over mountain roads to the crater.

When we arrived at the outer gates of the test area our credentials were examined by the Army guard. It was there I found out we had had a close call because we were late arriving over the crater.

The guard told us that, while we were flying over the area, we were constantly in the sights of the anti-aircraft guns. One of the outposts reported to headquarters that someone was "getting nosey" and they had us in the sights and asked instructions as to what to do. Of course, they were immediately informed the flight over the area was authorized, but it made us feel a little ill when we heard the story.

After being cleared by the guard at the gate, we proceeded to the crater itself. Dr. Bainbridge and I spent about an hour and a half arranging the program which we transcribed while the doctor and I were standing in the actual crater created by the bomb. Dr. Bainbridge told us the bomb, when it was detonated, had been placed on a 100 foot section of a 200 foot radar tower. One of the most amazing things to me was that the tower was completely vaporized by the heat and force of the Atomic Bomb.

There were four stubs of the tower sticking out of the ground approximately 12 inches that looked as though they had been cut off by an acetylene torch. The concrete footing of the tower was protruding from the ground because earth was blown out from around it.

Dr. Bainbridge told me during the course of our interview the heat created by the detonation registered in millions of degrees Fahrenheit, and that was the explanation for the green, crystalized area around the crater. Sandy soil was melted by the heat and flowed like lava. Finally, cooled in the desert air and turned to crystal.

I was fortunate enough to obtain a piece of the crystalized sand and hope you will all have the opportunity to see it at the end of this program.

Dr. Bainbridge controlled the detonation mechanism from what they called "South ten thousand" -- which was approximately six miles from the crater. It was a dugout affair with a huge instrument panel on which various reactions of the bomb were recorded. Dr. Bainbridge and his entire staff wore welder's glasses to enable them to watch the explosion without injury to their eyes.

Captain Howard Bush, the Army Commander in charge at the site, gave me one of the most interesting reactions to the explosion. He was at the "South Ten Thousand" with Dr. Bainbridge at the time of the detonation. He was, however, outside the sheltered area and was sitting on the ground with his back to the bomb.

At the instant of the detonation, Captain Bush said he had to feel of his eyes to see if they were closed because of the intense light. Because of the intensity of the light, he buried his eyes in his arms but still could see the light. He finally buried his arms in his legs but still could see light.

I was surprised to get everyone's reaction on the sound of the detonation. It was not the terrific noise that one would suspect. More of a dull thud and a sudden rush of wind. Some of the authorities say that a wind front of 750 miles an hour was set up by the explosion. However, it rapidly diminished over a distance of approximately five miles.

The green, crystalized area around the crater intrigued all of us. The surface is approximately one-half inch in thickness and very brittle -- cracked somewhat like sleet under our feet. We wore protection on our feet to guard us against radio activity.

Radio activity is what science calls gamma rays which radiate off the stone. You will later in the program have an opportunity to hear Dr. Bainbridge as I interviewed him on another phase of the crater.

Completing the program at the crater, we started to the Army Camp which is located on the site some twelve miles from the crater. On the way to the Army Camp we stopped off to view the ranch house in which the Atomic Bomb was assembled for the test. The windows of the ranch house were all blown in. The suction created pulled all the ceilings down into the rooms. This ranch house will probably live in history as a historic monument to the Atomic Bomb.

Upon arriving at the Army Camp we were treated to a fine steak dinner. Might say at this point that the Army at all times is the world's most perfect host in cooperating with correspondents in any way they could.

We set up our transcribing equipment in the Mess Hall at the Camp to transcribe the program getting the reactions of the Army men who had the gigantic task of guarding the security of the Atomic Bomb. This, as you know, was the most closely guarded secret of the United States Government during the war.

These boys, for a while, did not know what they were guarding. Finally, as experiments started taking shape, they were informed just what their task was. These boys remained in the area twelve months without contact with the outside world.

While we are speaking of security, the RKO Radio Pictures' "First Yank Into Tokyo" shows, in fiction form, the lengths to which our government went to obtain and secure the vital secret of the Atomic Bomb.

This Camp is one of the most completely equipped in the country -- having all types of recreational equipment, the best in food and all other facilities required by an army. The post also had one of the most complete weather stations in the world. The two meteorologists who predicted the weather for the scientists were the two men who set D-Day in Europe. Weather was one of the most important factors in conducting the test. The test was originally scheduled for two A. M. that morning, but was delayed to 5:22 A. M. because of a change of weather.

Captain Bush, during the course of the program, informed me that he and Dr. Bainbridge were at the tower with the bomb up to twenty minutes before it was detonated. While driving into camp we noticed poles and hundreds of wires on both sides of the road. Dr. Bainbridge told us these were the wires which controlled the scientific instruments during the test.

I had an opportunity to talk to most of the boys at the camp. They all gave me somewhat the same sort of story as Captain Bush. The main feature, as far as they were concerned, was the extreme light created.

To give a well rounded picture of the story, I decided to get the reaction of the people in Socorro, New Mexico, the town of approximately 4,000 people and which is located some thirty to thirty-five air-line miles from the crater. We set up our portable transcribing equipment in front of the post office in the typical New Mexico town. The transcription you will hear later.

On this transcription is the voice of Mr. Greene, whose daughter -- although totally blind -- and some seventy miles from the explosions actually saw the light created by the bomb. She was driving with her brother-in-law from Socorro to Albuquerque at the time of the explosion.

I talked to one man in Socorro who was blown from his bed by the force of the explosion. Everyone I talked to was awakened by the sound of the explosion. The residents of this town could see the smoke created by the explosion and which rose some 40,000 feet into the air.

I know that you, as well as myself and everyone else, are extremely interested in the size of this Atomic Bomb. The only reaction I could obtain was from Dr. Bainbridge and the only thing he would say was that the bomb was no minature.

After seeing the effect of the explosion of the Atomic Bomb I personally feel there is only one way open to us and that is some type of world authority to control it. If that is done, I believe it could become a weapon for peace and not the most destructive mechanism every created by man.

Now to give you further information on the Atomic Bomb, I am going to play for you the transcription released to the coast-to-coast network of the American Broadcasting Company by KRNT. During the playing of this transcription you will hear the actual transcription made from the air, the interview with Dr. Bainbridge and the interview with Mr. Greene, father of the blind girl who saw the light of the explosion.

AUTHOR'S NOTE: The following message was in the file that Cremeens donated to the White Sands Missile Range Public Affairs Office. It is labeled "The AP-WX Sept 15, 1945." It appears to be a teletype message sent by the Associated Press News Service to all of its subscribers and not just KRNT in Des Moines. Like the typical teletype message it is in all caps – we had one in the Public Affairs Office for years. The date is the same day Cremeens left Des Moines for Albuquerque.

NOTE TO EDITORS—(CONFIDENTIAL – NOT FOR PUBLICATION OR BROADCAST):

WASHINGTON—THE WAR DEPARTMENT HAS ISSUED THE FOLLOWING NOTE:
THE FOLLOWING MEMORANDUM IS CONFIDENTIAL AND NOT FOR PUBLICATION:
THE PRESIDENT OF THE UNITED STATES TODAY MADE THE FOLLOWING REQUEST FOR THE COOPERATION OF AMERICAN EDITORS AND BROADCASTERS AND THE PUBLIC IN PROTECTING THE SECRET OF THE ATOMIC BOMB. THE PRESIDENT SAID THAT HIS ACTION WAS IN THE NATIONAL INTEREST AND NOT WITH ANY IDEA OF IMPOSING CENSORSHIP UPON THE PRESS OR RADIO.
THE REQUEST, HEREWITH COMMUNICATED TO YOU IN CONFIDENCE, IS AS FOLLOWS:

"IN THE INTEREST OF THE HIGHEST NATIONAL SECURITY, EDITORS AND BROADCASTERS ARE REQUESTED TO WITHHOLD INFORMATION (BEYOND THE OFFICIAL RELEASES) WITHOUT FIRST CONSULTING WITH THE WAR DEPARTMENT, CONCERNING SCIENTIFIC PROCESSES, FORMULAS, AND MECHANICS OF OPERATIONS AND TECHNIQUES EMPLOYED IN THE OPERATIONAL USE OF THE ATOMIC BOMB: LOCATION, PROCUREMENT AND CONSUMPTION OF URANIUM SOCKS (sic): QUALITY AND QUANTITY STOCKS: QUALITY AND QUANTITY OF PRODUCTION OF THESE BOMBS: THEIR PHYSICS AND CHARACTERISTICS: AND INFORMATION AS TO THE RELATIVE IMPORTANCE OF THE VARIOUS METHODS OR PLANTS, OR OF THEIR RELATIVE FUNCTIONS OR EFFICIENCIES."

AUTHOR'S NOTE: George Cremeens had to be one of the first tourists to pick up Trinitite at Ground Zero. In fact, one of the government photos of him at the site shows him stooping and picking up a piece of the glass as he poses for the camera. We don't know if the reporters and photographers who visited with Gen. Groves were able to grab some chunks or not – probably not with the number of security folks there as well as Groves and Oppenheimer being on hand to warn folks off. We know Cremeens got a piece because of this letter from Bainbridge and the fact that Cremeens used it in his "show and tell" programs about his visit.

September 20, 1945

Dear Mr. Cremeens:

I am writing you to re-emphasize the possible danger to you or others from the glass which you, Capt. Rutherford and your technician secured at the atomic bomb test site last Monday, September 17. You picked up this glassy material near the center of the crater where some radioactive material had been blown into the ground because of the low height of the test bomb above the ground.

The glass should under no circumstances be put into jewelry of any kind, particularly bracelets or necklaces where it would be close to the skin, as radioactive materials in the glass might produce burns similar to those produced by X-rays. A less dangerous disposition of this material would be to mount it in a glass jar so that it could not be handled and so that no one would spend more than a short time close to it.

I cannot be responsible for this after it has left my hands and request that you and your associates take the necessary precautions. I recommend that this should not leave your custody or control.

Mr. Anderson and I trust that you obtained what you wanted on your visit.

With kindest regards,

Yours sincerely,
K.T. Bainbridge

AUTHOR'S NOTE: For his four radio shows in Des Moines, Cremeens created large pre-recorded segments of interviews and descriptions that he simply introduced each evening. These are the four scripts he used for the "live" introductions to the pieces. The formatting differs from night to night and the script has several typos.

<u>MONDAY, SEPTEMBER 24, 1945, 8:30 to 8:45 p.m.</u>

Good evening, ladies and gentlemen. This is George Cremeens speaking from the studios of KRNT. Tonight KRNT presents the first radio broadcast made in and around the test area of the world's first Atomic Bomb.

Saturday morning, September 15th, Frank Ligouri, KRNT Sound Technician, and I left Des Moines, by plane, and flew to Albuquerque, New Mexico. Basing in Albuquerque, and flying to the locations at which the broadcasts were transcribed, we obtained four programs designed to give you a complete picture of the test.

The test was made in Oscura Basin, New Mexico, some 170 miles from Albuquerque, New Mexico. Tonight's broadcast was made while flying over the crater. Our pilot, Captain Rutherford, Wing Commander of the Oskaloosa, Iowa, Civil Air Patrol, circled the crater area to enable us to transcribe a description.

Our Sound Engineer worked under great difficulty due to the fact it was necessary for us to supply power to our recording machine with a battery driven roto generator. To reduce noise of the motor, it was necessary for us to keep the windows closed. To further reduce the noise, I covered myself and the microphone with a leather jacket. Now by wire recording we take you to Oscura Basin, New Mexico....
(TRANSCRIBED PROGRAM)

We sincerely hope that through this series of broadcasts on the test of the world's first Atomic Bomb we can succeed in giving our listeners further information on this greatest discovery in the history of mankind. The next broadcast in this series will be a broadcast originating in the actual crater made by the detonation of the Atomic Bomb.

On the broadcast you will hear the voice of Dr. K.T. Bainbridge, the scientist in charge of selecting the site and setting up the necessary installations for the Atomic Bomb test.

This program came to you as a Special Events feature of KRNT.

<u>WEDNESDAY, SEPT. 26, 1945, 9:45-10:00</u>

Good evening Ladies and Gentlemen this is George Cremeens speaking from the studies of KRNT. This evening we present the second program in an exclusive series of broadcasts on the test of the World's first Atomic Bomb

Tonight's program originates in the crater created by the Atomic Bomb. Because of the crater's isolated location, it was necessary for us to use a battery driven Roto-Generator to supply power for our wire recorder. Our sound technician Frank Lagouri set up our equipment in an army car near the crater. You will notice at various times during the program a rustling noise created by the wind blowing into our mike.

Here Ladies and gentlemen by means of wire recording is the first broadcast to originate from the Atomic Bomb test area.

(Program) (13:40)

Through this series of exclusive broadcasts KRNT is endeavoring to give it's listeners a well rounded insight on the test of the Atomic Bomb. Tomorrow evening at 8:30 we will present a program originating in the Mess Hall of the Army headquarters on the test site. The voice of Capt. Howard Bush, Army commander on the scene will be heard on tomorrow evenings broadcast.

This program came to you as a Public service feature of KRNT.

SEPT. 27, 1945, 8:30 – 8:45

Good-evening ladies and gentlemen this is George Cremeens speaking from the studios of KRNT. Tonight we present the third program in an exclusive series of broadcasts direct from the test area of the world's first Atomic Bomb. This program was transcribed Monday Sept. 17th. The delay in presenting this program was made necessary, due to the fact all of these Atomic Bomb broadcasts had to be cleared for broadcast by the War Department.

Now we take you to Oscura Basin New Mexico.....

(Program)

Tune in Saturday evening 8:30 to 8:55 P.M. for the final program in this series of broadcasts, the first to originate from the Atomic Bomb test area.

This program cam to you as a pubic service feature of KRNT.

NO DATE OR TIME ARE LISTED FOR THIS FINAL SCRIPT

Good evening, ladies and gentlemen. This is George Cremeens speaking from the studios of KRNT. Tonight we present the fourth and last in a series of exclusive broadcasts made in and around the atomic bomb test area in New Mexico. We have endeavored through this series of programs to bring our listeners a well rounded picture of both the scientific and human reaction to the world's first atomic bomb. Tonight's program origi-

nates in Socorro, New Mexico, a town of 4,000 population, located some 35 air miles from the bomb crater. Immediately following this broadcast, we will present a digest of newspaper, radio, and magazine opinion as expressed by the nation's leading commentaries and editorialists on the subject "What should be done with the Atomic Bomb?" Now by wire recording we take you to Socorro, New Mexico
(Program-13:25)

From the residence of Socorro, New Mexico, you have heard reactions in this town located some 35 air miles from the crater.

Now for a digest of newspaper, radio, and magazine opinion on what should be done with the atomic bomb.....

Some Sources

Books

Atom Bombs - The Top Secret Inside Story of Little Boy and Fat Man by John Coster-Mullen.

City Of Fire – Los Alamos and the Atomic Age, 1943-1945 by James W Kunetka.

Day of Trinity by Lansing Lamont.

Day One – Before Hiroshima And After by Peter Wyden.

The Day the Sun Rose Twice by Ferenc Morton Szasz.

Manhattan: The Army And The Atomic Bomb by Vincent C. Jones.

Men And Atoms by William L. Laurence.

Now It Can Be Told by Lieutenant General Leslie R. Groves.

Tales of Tomorrow #1: Invaders at Ground Zero by David Houston.

The Making Of The Atomic Bomb by Richard Rhodes.

These Hallowed Grounds. A Pursuit Of American History by Debora Busenkell and Richard Busenkell.

Trinity's Children: Living Along America's Nuclear Highway by Scott McCartney.

Magazines and Journals

American Heritage Of Invention & Technology

Health Physics

New Mexico Magazine

Nuclear Weapons Journal

Polo: Players' Edition Magazine

Reports

Health Physics Survey of Trinity Site by Frederic Fey, Los Alamos Scientific Laboratory, 1967.

Los Alamos 1943-1945: The Beginning of an Era. Los Alamos publication LASL-79-78.

Project Trinity 1945-1946 by Carl Maag and Steve Rohrer for the U.S. Defense Nuclear Agency.

Radiological Survey and Evaluation of the Fallout Area from the Trinity Test: Chupadera Mesa and White Sands Missile Range, New Mexico Los Alamos.

Trinity by Kenneth Barinbridge. Los Alamos publication LA-6300-H.

Miscellaneous

Integration of the Holloman – White Sands Missile Test Ranges 1947 – 1952
    An Air Research and Development Command Historical Monogaph.
Life at Trinity Base Camp by Thomas Merlan.
Nuclear Files Archive – a website at: http://www.nuclearfiles.org/docs
Pit Assembly Crew Interviews by Alice Buck, September 1983. Department of Energy McDonald Ranch House Project.
Pursuit of Plutonium by Dave Rudolph.
The Trinity Experiments by Thomas Merlan.
Thermal Effects Of Atomic bomb Explosions On Soils At Trinity And Eniwitok by Eugene Staritzky, June 13, 1950. LA-1126.
Letters and documents from the Schmidt family, Marvin Davis Sr., Carl Rudder, and George Cremeens.
Lots of interviews and just shooting the breeze with the many scientists and support personnel who visited Trinity from 1977 to the present.

Made in the USA
Columbia, SC
25 September 2024